The Birth of an Ecovillage

Adventures in an alternative world

by Paul Wimbush

Published in 2012 by FeedARead Publishing

Illustrations by Paul Wimbush

British Library C.I.P.

A CIP catalogue record for this title is available from the British Library.

This book is dedicated to Hoppi, my gorgeous wife, and my three children: Jarvis, Jarro and Emba, all of whom have had to come to terms with having quite a wacky dad.

I would like to thank to all those who took a bold leap of faith and believed in the Lammas project.

‘Ar bo ben bid bont’

Attributed to Bendigeidfran
from the Welsh Epic ‘The Mabinogion’

Translated from Welsh – ‘He who is at the head, let him be a bridge’

Introduction

I live in an ecovillage. I am not talking about a suburb with solar panels, or a community with a car-share scheme. By ecovillage I mean a collective of households pioneering a new culture centered around sustainable living. We are transforming a depleted landscape into a mosaic of biodiverse ecologies in which human beings become an intrinsic part of the natural world. We are building funky homes using natural or recycled materials and creating an economy based on land-based micro enterprises. It is only a small ecovillage at the moment, and it is in its early years. Nonetheless it sets a precedent that challenges the way our society relates to our landbase.

This book is one perspective on the people, places and events that led to the creation of the Lammas ecovillage in West Wales. In sharing my story I have tried to reflect the truth as best I can, in the hope that some insight might be gained from my experiences. It is also your story, because if there is one truth to which this age will in time testify, it is that all things are connected.

My tale is that of an ordinary man in an extraordinary time. It is difficult to be objective about the culture in which we live. I personally needed to step outside of mainstream culture to appreciate where we are and where we have come from. I believe that in years to come people will reflect upon this period of history with utter disbelief. Our society is consuming and destroying the very environment upon which we depend for life. In so doing, we are dismantling ecosystems of complexity and wonder beyond comprehension. At the same time we crowd around our television screens to watch pictures of the last pockets of pristine wilderness before they disappear. We are hypnotised and disempowered, caught in the illusion of retail economies. And yet it is in the darkest hour that the potential for redemption is strongest.

I grew up in a middle-class family in a suburban village in Berkshire. It was a very secure and loving upbringing. It was also fairly unremarkable. I watched television, played football with friends and wore school uniform. In my teens I rebelled by drinking copious amounts of beer and listening to rock music. Then something happened. Something began to shift in me. Through the noise and chatter of modern life I discerned a new voice. Hints of deeper meaning. Whispers from another world. Coincidences questioned and intuitions acknowledged. I was led away.

Chapter 1
Tipi Valley; Discovery

14th July 1992, Country lanes north of Merthyr Tydfil

I had been on the road for four days and had settled into a routine of walking and camping. My enormous, clumsy rucksack was testament to the fact that I had no idea what I was doing. My feet were sore and my body ached. My clothes were either too bulky and would cause me to sweat, or they were too light and I would get soaked when it rained. Once again I reassured myself that this was a good idea. It was surely better than hanging around in Cardiff when all my other student friends had headed off home for the summer break. I had thought that I would enjoy the walk. Gravity conspired with my backpack to persuade me otherwise.

I had seen very little traffic that day and held out my thumb to passing cars more as an experiment in openness rather than out of any serious intent to hitch a lift. After being ignored for several hours I was surprised when a small crowded hatchback stopped and, after a brief flurry of activity, I was bundled into the car, being questioned for directions. It became clear that the Dutch driver was hopelessly lost and was desperately trying to resolve the situation by driving very fast and taking random turns at road junctions. One of the passengers explained that they had been driving through Welsh country lanes for over an hour. With my huge rucksack on my lap, I struggled to unfold my map. Within minutes we had whizzed past a number of crossroads and, what with the steamed up windows and my rucksack blocking my view, I was struggling to identify anything other than blurred hedge-banks. After several attempts to locate where we were on my map, I reluctantly accepted that I had lost my bearings. I clamoured to be let out. The driver muttered something in frustration as I squeezed out of the car. Having deposited me by the roadside he sped away and I slumped onto my backpack, questioning what I was doing; "It would help", I thought, "if it was clearer where I was going!" My destination was not marked on any map. I knew that it existed some distance north of a town called Llandeilo. I was heading for the mythical Tipi Valley.

Whenever I considered what I was doing I felt something between anticipation and apprehension. I was trusting my journey to a crazy-eyed traveller I had met some years back on Silbury Hill in Wiltshire. His directions were all I had to go on. I had been inspired by his description of a community of wild hippies living a carefree life at one with nature deep in the Welsh hills. Apparently there was a place called the 'Big-lodge', in which people could come and stay for free. This wondrous story had stayed with me over the years and now, in a way that felt quite out of character, I was on a mission to discover if such a place really existed.

~

16th July 1992, the Black Mountain

As I reached the brow of the forestry track, the full majesty of the Black Mountain revealed itself to me. The sweeping arcs of the peaks towered graciously above rolling plains of moor and marsh, bracken and gorse. Patches of sunlight raced across the undulating landscape, highlighting the gulleys and rises. In the distance I could see clusters of miniature sheep and horses scattered across the land. It was as if I had stepped back in time to find myself in some wild prehistoric landscape. The sky above me grew dark and heavy grey clouds unleashed an icy hailstorm. As I scrabbled for my waterproofs I was pelted by the heavens. The warm summer's day had momentarily transformed into winter. It was as if the mountain had sent out a message of power. I felt humbled, and looked around for cover. There was none. I pressed on, cold and wet, and feeling very, very small.

~

18th July 1992, Cwmdu, near Llandeilo

I stopped at a dilapidated farmhouse to ask directions from an old, toothless farmer. With a gleam in his eye he motioned a huge arc across the sky with his arm as he described how he had once seen a wigwam blown away in a storm. "Is this the way?" I asked. "It is, you need to follow this road and turn left at the crossroads." he said. A smile crept across his face. "You'll be in for some fun! They walk around totally naked in the summer and share each others wives you know!"

~

18th July 1992, the Moor, Tipi Valley

Dusk was beginning to set as I arrived at what should have been my destination. I stood back and examined the conical tent. "This can't be right", I thought. "It's not big for a start." But I was exhausted and keen to relieve myself from the deadweight of my rucksack. The last hill had almost finished me off, or rather the muddy path that wound its way up it. I mused again over the scrambled set of directions which had been thrown at me by the children. Their ambush had begun well, with what must have been a satisfying look of horror on my face. In truth my reaction was more to do with the muddy faces, wild hair and torn clothes of the ambush party rather than their home-made bows and arrows with which I had been threatened. When it became clear that I was not going to be giving any money away they largely lost interest. After trudging through 'the village field', over the bridge and up 'the motorway' (what did that mean?) I had spotted a small tipi on the moor and despite its obvious shortcomings, was hopeful that I had at last arrived. Curiosity propelled me forward; I had never seen a tipi before. I pushed aside the small canvas door and stooped to peer in. Inside the decor was fairly minimal, yet appeared surprisingly comfortable. There was a fireplace in the middle of the circle and a bed laid out at the back. To the left were some baskets of clothes and to the right some metal trunks and kitchenware. The floor was covered in rugs and sheepskins and there were a few personal bags and effects scattered around. "Could this really be the Big-lodge?" I asked myself. Feeling edgy at the possibility of intruding on someone's private space, and at the same time exhausted from the day's hike, I decided to take the risk and go inside. Once I had squeezed through the small doorway and sat down, I was surprised by how cosy it was. Taking out my camping-gas stove I cooked up my customary meal of rice and dried soup mix (the most lightweight food I could think of). The familiar tasteless sludge was welcome. The night began to close in. I resolved to press on, convinced on reflection that this was not the Big-lodge. Feeling like a lost stranger I headed off into the dusk towards a wooded area from which I could hear what sounded like wood being chopped, to ask directions.

~

August 1992, Neil's roundhouse, Middle Earth, Tipi Valley

"All the Earth is sacred, every step we take.
All the air is sacred, every breath we take.
Unite the people, we are one.
Unite the people, we are one."

The heavy beat filled the space. Candlelight defined the circle of focused people, crammed together two or three deep around the smoky fire. The rhythm was ancient. The people drifted in and out of a trance of remembrance. The heavy set expressions of the people seemed as crude as their attire: predominantly wool and leather. Outside the roundhouse the drumming resounded across the landscape. Smoke filtered through the thatched roof, and the lights from distant farms provided the only clue to the modern age. The Earth received the rhythm with a longing gratitude, its precious touch caressing her body. I felt honoured to be welcomed here. The beat continued long into the night, searching, remembering.

~

August 1992, Big-lodge summer pitch, Tipi Valley

I leaned into the backrest, welcoming the gentle warmth of the evening sun on my face as I listened to the sound of a flute echoing in the valley. In front of me a merry fire was heating up a large cauldron of water which was to be used for cooking and washing clothes. The sides of the Big-lodge had been rolled up to give the space some light and air. I had spent the afternoon collecting reeds from the bog, and the floor was now dressed with a fresh layer of green. Across from me, a fellow Big-lodge resident, 'Rabbit', was sewing his new tipi cover using a small hand powered sewing machine while Mark, another potential tipi-convert, was cutting vegetables for the evening meal. I felt connected to the land here in a way that was completely new to me. A depth of belonging that warmed my heart.

~

Right from the moment I arrived in Tipi Valley I was deeply touched by the people and their way of life, though it took a good few weeks for the initial culture-shock to wear off. I began to get used to life without lights, stereos and hot running water. Admittedly I would venture off to the nearest town at any opportunity to get a 'hit' of fish and chips, chocolate and newspapers. And yet on returning to the valley I could feel myself relax. I began to get used to lighting fires, washing in the stream and living in a tipi. I stayed in the Big-lodge all summer and grew close to the other people staying there. I did find living in a communal space somewhat wearing. In some ways it was akin to living in a goldfish bowl. It was a small price to pay for the chance to live as a part of the tribe. I rejoiced in finding some truth and meaning in this life. The deep connection of these people to their environment was an inspiration and I had never come across anything like it before. It was an awakening for me.

I returned to Cardiff in October 1992, though I felt as if I had left my spirit behind. I then completed my degree in Architecture, and subsequently worked for nine months to pay off my student debts and save some money to buy my first tipi. With great joy I returned to the valley in the spring of 1994.

The land in Tipi Valley is relatively high (about 220 metres above sea level) and encompasses a range of habitats from exposed moor-land to temperate woodland. The soil is acidic and poor and the weather is predominantly windy and wet (averaging about 2.4 metres of rainfall each year).

Tipi Valley was established in the seventies on land sold to hippies by two liberal minded farmers. Over the years it had grown slowly and steadily. When I came to live there, it had evolved into three distinct zones. 'The top' was an area in which about twenty households lived in a colourful array of mobile dwellings and caravans in various states of stasis. 'Middle Earth' was a relatively new development of five households on about twenty acres. People there lived in thatched huts and tipis. This area had been created as a permaculture project and an abundance of young trees were testament to the impending conversion from field to forest garden. 'The bottom' was for me the heart of Tipi Valley. Set in about a hundred acres with no vehicular access, it was in this area that the tipi culture was strongest. About twenty five households lived there under canvas. The land had originally been farmland, though after twenty years of regeneration and intimate care had become a diverse patchwork of woodland, scrub and glade. It was literally alive with nature spirits.

There was an unwritten culture in the valley which served to bind and root its inhabitants. This culture had evolved over many years and was a fusion of conventional and alternative social ethics, Native American tradition, loopholes in the planning law and a dialogue with the land itself. It covered many aspects of behaviour ranging from etiquette to taboo and included rules, traditions and customs.

The rules had evolved over time and covered the absolute basics of living lightly on the land. They included a ban on dogs; which came from a respect for farming neighbours who had lost too many lambs to free-range dogs in the early days. There was also a ban on benders (a simple framed tent) due to a historic association with permanent tents becoming a health liability through accumulating rubbish and attracting rodents. There were also some basic hygiene guidelines such as not using soap in the stream and burying all human poo.

Permanence was heavily frowned upon in Tipi Valley, with good reason. Human beings inevitably impact upon a natural landscape, even when living lightly on the Earth. If you move every six months nature restores the land to a natural radiance. The pathways that people etch into the land fade and disappear, compost heaps rot down and are reclaimed by undergrowth. The tradition of moving your home every six months meant that at moving time, when you came across that book/ item of clothing/ piece of kitchenware that you hadn't used since you last hauled it 500 yards across the stream and up the hill, the temptation to get rid of it often won over the 'just in case it will come in handy' niggle. Thus tipi folk generally kept only a minimum of possessions. It was a great discipline to embrace and one that has since remained with me.

Every winter the tipis would gather together in the village fields, where we would share the challenges that winter brought. In the summer people would move up the hill onto their summer pitches where their gardens were. These tended to consist of a series of terraced cultivated beds with an area for fruit bushes and trees. They all contained compost-making areas which processed bracken and food waste to create soil. Some of the more established gardens had small polytunnels or greenhouses.

One of the key traditions was to maintain an attitude of respect for immediate neighbours. If you were contemplating an action such as moving to a new pitch, creating a garden or making a woodpile, the protocol was that you would check this out with anybody neighbouring the place which you were considering for your activity. During the run-up to 'moving time' there was a flurry of social activity as people worked out where they would live next.

Media coverage was actively discouraged within the tribe, to the point where even taking photos was somewhat taboo. The thinking behind this was that the best way to avoid interference from bureaucratic officialdom was to keep a low-profile.

Many of the tipi folk collected state-benefits, reasoning that it was completely justified to accept any government hand-outs that were on offer. I did claim some benefits for the first year until, inspired by some of the more self-reliant tipi folk, I decided against it. I then developed other ways of generating income. A few times a year I would embark with friends on busking tours in town centres across the UK. I enjoyed playing folk music, though found the urban experience draining. My preferred income stream was to sell art and craft work at the summer festivals. I would paint animal totems and celtic-knotwork patterns onto canvas shields. Thus I earned enough to meet my minimal needs.

Most of the time a peaceful order was maintained in the valley, with the ways of the tribe being passed on verbally to new members. Occasionally situations would stray into unacceptable realms and action was called for. I recall one domestic violence incident, a couple of occasions where unstable characters in the Big-lodge had outstayed their welcome, and a few incidents of drug dealing; all of which required a strong-arm approach. There was a particular clan of Scottish men who acted as an internal force when required. They were not to be messed with.

The history of the evolution of Tipi Valley is a story in its own right. In the early days small parcels of land were purchased 'on tick' with hippies paying farmers five pounds each week. On completion the deeds were assigned to a 'land trust' for safekeeping. Slowly the population and land area grew, with various factions that threatened the viability or integrity of the whole being driven out. Ric the Vic, a long-standing resident (and ordained vicar) has kept an archive of the social evolution of the valley. He was a well-respected elder in the tribe and often acted as an interface with the wider world. By the time I had arrived, Tipi Valley was largely established and Carmarthenshire County Council had, following years of legal action, seemingly given up trying to evict the illegal settlement.

~

October 1994, Triangle field, Tipi Valley

Woodsmoke drifted lazily across the village fields as the morning sounds of wood being chopped and children playing mingled with the smells of porridge and coffee. I had stepped outside to stretch in the morning sunshine when I caught the awkward movements out of the corner of my eye. To my astonishment two men in suits and anoraks were nervously stepping over the stile into the field carrying clipboards. Having crossed the bridge they hesitated on the near bank, looking at the unfamiliar scene before them. By now a few of the tribe had stopped what they were doing and were watching them with a mixture of disbelief and reservation. The domestic background noise ceased, the lazy morning feeling being quickly displaced by a territorial tension.

I assumed that they must be from the Council, probably planners. The two men faltered and after a quick exchange between themselves, scribbled a note on their clipboards, then turned around and hastily departed. A gentle chuckle filled the air and the lazy morning was resumed.

~

January 1995, Alex's lodge, Triangle field, Tipi Valley

The icy rain hammered on the tipi's canvas cover whilst we sat inside, snug and warm around the fire. A cast-iron kettle, recently emptied into the tin bath, was re-hung on a chain over the fire, heating water for the next round of domestic tasks. In the doorway, two small children played in the steaming bath whilst their mother was busy sorting through a clothes basket. I was engrossed in the book of herb-lore that she had loaned me. The fire crackled, the children chattered and as she busied herself she sang;

"I find my joy in the simple things that come from the Earth.
I find my joy in the sun that shines and the water that sings to me.
Listen to the wind and listen to the water.
Hear what they say.
Singing heya, heya, heya, heya, heya, heya ho"

I felt blessed to be there.

~

To survive and thrive in tipi culture required an ordered discipline. Tipis, or 'lodges' varied in size from a 14 feet diameter (for a single person) to an 18 footer (big family lodge) and a common pattern of layout existed through necessity as much as through tradition. Upon entering a lodge (which usually involved stooping though a simple and often leaky doorway) there was the porch area in which shoes, or more usually wellies, were removed and stored. In winter, when socialising was necessary to keep the 'cabin fever' from setting in, even a small lodge could have up to eight visitors. The porch area could very easily disappear under a scrum of muddy wellies, making leaving the lodge with any grace impossible. After the Christmas party in the Big lodge, when the wellie scrum assumed epic proportions, it was customary to adopt any pair of wellies which fit, (invariably the last person to leave would end up with two left footed wellies of different sizes!) Whilst the porch area was generally gravelled, the rest of the lodge would be covered with rushes and topped with a thick carpet of sheepskins. Possessions were stored at the back of the lodge, creating a free space around the fire for movement. During the day, beds would be rolled up to create backrests. On one side of the porch would be a wood storage area, along with a chopping block and small axe. On the other side would be the kitchen area, with food generally stored in tin trunks for security (from small hungry creatures). Water would be collected from the stream and stored in large containers near the doorway (in case of spillage).

Collecting wood was a daily task, summer and winter with most households gathering it by hand from the surrounding countryside. On principle most tipi folk did not cut 'green' (living) wood for fuel. This was in order to allow the land, which had previously been overgrazed pasture, to regenerate. There was a practical aspect to this as well, in that the smoke from a green-wood fire is generally intolerable. Dead-wood was thus a scarce commodity around the settlement. I learnt quickly that it was necessary to become very skilled at finding dead-wood if I wanted to avoid walking miles each day to gather fuel. The key was in spotting 'standing' dead-wood, which are branches which have died and are still attached to the tree. These branches remain fairly dry due to their elevation and are far more desirable than those which have fallen to the ground to become damp.

During my first winter there, water fell from the sky in some form (rain, drizzle, mist, snow, hail) every day for two months. As well as being depressing it was physically very challenging to live in such conditions under canvas. Keeping myself dry and my possessions mould-free involved a life that literally revolved around the fire. The ability to light and nurture fire becomes a lifeline in these circumstances. Of all the people who visited the valley, only the very committed and the very capable stayed. A visitor's first winter was considered an initiation process.

Living with fire became such an integral part of my life that I began to appreciate a world of subtleties which must have been common knowledge to our ancestors. A hawthorn fire will burn bright and long and will feature a colourful flame with red, green and purple flecks. A willow fire, however, is yellow, bright, quick to burn and will 'spit' embers. Ash will burn hot under any conditions whereas mountain ash is reluctant to burn at all. I learnt many things with the tipi tribe; the art of foraging for wild food, the craft of curing animal skins, how to grow fruit and vegetables, the subtleties of nature's ways, how to appreciate all the seasons, and how to party. The tipi people knew how to party.

Some say that Tipi Valley originated in the sixties when hippies wanted a location to carry on partying when all the summer festivals had finished. Partying at Tipi Valley was a craft. A party would be cultivated, nurtured and encouraged. It would peak when it was designed to peak and it would pause when it was designed to pause. A good party was a group journey into the joy of abandonment. The heart to any party was in the celebration of life through music and song. There was a wide range of beautiful songs and chants which were sung at gatherings.

The songs were an important part of the tipi culture – an expression of thanks for the heart connection that bonded the human world to the natural world. There was a genuine sense of paradise found amongst the tribe, a thankfulness for the opportunity to live barefoot amongst the trees, plants and animals.

~

March 1995, Village field, Tipi Valley

"Cauldron of changes, feather on the bone," Irish Steve's clear voice cut through the evening air. He was sitting and drumming on his djembe and the gathering

of people couldn't help but respond to the invitation. Voices and drums joined in;

"Hawk of eternity, bringer of the stones.
We are the old people. We are the new people.
We are the same people, wiser than before."
Over and over the chant intoned.

~

If there was a chief to the Tipi tribe, that honour would have fallen to 'Irish Steve', whose passion for the tipi village has been a beacon for many. He was a charismatic leader with a deep commitment to living lightly on the Earth. With his partner he raised three children under canvas, and somehow embodied the art of tent living. He was both welcoming and hostile, an untameable free spirit.

There was one man, however, whose approach particularly inspired me. Pete left his dairy farm when in his forties to go and live with the hippies. His angle has always erred to the agricultural rather than the hunter-gatherer. By the time I came to live in Tipi Valley, Pete had effectively built a smallholding on a steep north-facing hillside. He was living in a small thatched roundhouse which could be dismantled and moved when necessary. He kept goats for milk and chickens for eggs. A moss-covered barn stored his willow supplies (for basketry), his hay and his tools. He grew virtually all of his own food on a series of cultivated terraces. The exceptions were flour, sugar, butter, coffee and rolled barley for the goats. What was most remarkable about his set-up was the beauty of it.

He managed to lay it out in such a manner that you only ever saw a fraction of it, the rest remaining hidden behind narrow screens of regenerating wilderness. He supported a family on one and a half acres of north-facing marginal land and he lived a very rich and comfortable life.

~

Full moon in October 1995, Sweat lodge summer site, Tipi Valley

The people had assembled around the sweatlodge fire. Drums drummed, whistles played and the tribe sang;

"The Earth is our mother,
We will take care of her,
Hey yunga, ho yunga, hey yung yung,
Hey yunga, ho yunga, hey yung yung,
We tread upon her sacred ground,
With every step we take..."

~

November 1995, Village field, Tipi Valley

A winter's night. The air was sharp and clear. A frost sparkled from the crystalline grass. The star-light reflected upon the magnificent arc of tipis. A warm glow of firelight and candle emanated from the cover of the Big-lodge. A gentle social hum came from the gathering inside. The beauty of the moment struck me. I felt completely a part of this tribe, a part of this Earth.

~

The Big-lodge was literally a huge tipi. It stood about ten metres tall and defined a majestic space. It acted as both a community hall and a guest house rolled into one. During the summer it often became home to a band of young people who were travelling through, visiting or considering living in the valley. Its dual role enabled people of the village to keep an eye on the visitors whilst popping in for a cup of tea and a catch-up on village news. It went through various cycles of being beautifully maintained to being completely 'lunched out' (abandoned). This depended in part on the morale of the settlement, and in part on the power and attitude of the guests that were staying there. Like all the other tipis, the Big-lodge was moved every six months. This was an enormous task, for each pole in itself was very heavy.

On rare occasions the Big-lodge was taken outside of the valley. One summer a group of us young tipi warriors took the Big-lodge to a 'rainbow gathering' in Scotland. The gathering of some several hundred 'eco warriors' took place on a windswept desolate moor, miles from any road or habitation. It was one of those remarkable events that went completely unnoticed by mainstream society and yet on some level held deep significance. On the surface it was a feat of endurance. Despite being midsummer, the weather was cold, wet and windy. We were plagued with clouds of midges. In the Big-lodge we adopted the approach of burning green wood with the smoke-flaps closed. From the outside you could see the smoke issuing from the lowest fringe of the tipi. The inside was smoky (which we were well used to) and, most importantly, midge free. Against all odds about a thousand people visited the gathering at its peak, sharing food, skills, a love of the Earth and a vision for an alternative future society.

I would return to England to visit my family regularly. I had a son, Jarvis, from a previous relationship and I endeavoured to maintain our close connection. When he was considered old enough, he would come and stay with me during the school holidays. It was not easy for him to adapt to the different culture, being used to television and processed food, however this eased over time.

After living at Tipi Valley for a year a friend from Cardiff, Jeni, came to live there too. She was a tall, Amazonian woman with an elegant poise. After a short while we fell in love and became partners. She had been studying music in Cardiff and quickly adapted her classical training on the cello to playing folk music on the fiddle. She learnt the necessary practical skills for tipi living with ease and before long was accepted as a native. It was good to have company, especially in the depths of winter.

~

Early December 1995, Triangle field, Tipi Valley

It was a freezing cold winter's morning. Jeni had, through feats of extreme stretching, managed to light a fire without getting out of bed and had placed our water containers near the fire so that we could thaw out some water to put in the kettle. I had laid there as long as I could but could resist no longer. I rushed out of bed, kicked open the door (which had frozen to the cover and was as stiff as a board) and went outside for a pee. To my astonishment I spotted Scilla, one of the elders, breaking the ice in the stream so that she could wash herself. Feeling my feet start to go numb on the frozen ground, I scuttled back inside and leapt into bed feeling a little ashamed at being so soft. Scilla always amazed me. Some years previously she had broken her back and had metal rods bolted to her spine for support. She was fiercely independent and kept a beautiful, model lodge.

~

Winter Solstice 1995, Scots pines, The Moor

The rain slammed into us as we huddled around the fire. We were at the highest point of the moor atop an ancient circular embankment crowned with two wizened scots pine trees. It was midwinter's night and we had gathered to hold vigil until dawn. We were wholly exposed to the ferocity of the elements. The wind howled at us through the darkest hour of the deepest night. A deep sombre rhythm from the damp drum and the occasional guttural chant reflected the determined focus of the vigil. A small fire burned amidst a scruffy collection of thorn branches, offering little respite from the wind and rain. Deep inside us we kept the inner flames alive. It was the only way to survive the biting cold. Nurturing the sacred fires within.

~

April 1996, Sacred Grove, Tipi Valley

I was sitting in the long grass. The leaves from the Oak and Sycamore trees cast a green hue upon the huge mossy boulders. The morning was misty and cool. There was a sadness in the land. The air was heavy. The birds were quiet. The animals were subdued. The water was still. There was a whisper on the breeze. "Great change will come."

~

June 1996, My summer pitch, Tipi Valley

I felt as if my heart was breaking. I stood in my garden, with half a sack of twigs abandoned at my feet. My feet were rooted to the ground. Despair overwhelmed me. Tears streamed down my face.
Whilst I was privileged to live in a small sheltered oasis, I was all too aware of the wider environmental destruction around me. I had watched huge areas mined for gravel and then backfilled with household waste. I had seen the urban sprawl grow and swallow field and woodland indiscriminately. The village in which I had grown up had been next to a nuclear warhead factory. I was aware of the ever growing traffic and had spent time at the Newbury road protest the previous winter. Our precious Earth was being torn apart in the name of progress. I had been a part of that culture. Waves of grief coursed through me.

~

Whilst challenging, life in the valley was equally rewarding. Enjoyment of the simple things in life comes naturally when the surroundings are so beautiful and the people around you are relaxed and happy. I embraced the lifestyle wholeheartedly and found great joy in the company of friends, nature and music. Cooking on an open fire required an increased focus on the present moment. I grew as much food as I could and also harvested from the area. This home-grown or wild food was often referred to as ‘power food’. I grew to appreciate that there was a particular harmony to food which had been grown in the same bioregion as its consumer, a resonance which through shared environmental influence imparted additional life giving properties. It seemed to me that this was enhanced further when an intimate relationship between the plant or animal and the person existed.

About once a fortnight I would go to Carmarthen town to purchase essentials (candles, flour, butter, bow-saw blades etc). This generally involved squashing into the back of Bob the Bus’s transit van on a Saturday morning along with many other hairy comrades clutching their empty rucksacks. After a dark, bumpy and smoky ride we would emerge bleary-eyed into a car-park in Carmarthen, somewhat surprised at the grey nature of the surroundings. Coping with the urban environment required me to energetically shut down and shield myself. Returning home brought palpable relief. Home was green, wild and free.

Next to tipi valley was a 20 acre conifer plantation, originally planted in the seventies when government subsidies encouraged pulp timber production. Over the years, by virtue of its proximity to the valley, it had been carefully harvested for both its young tree trunks (tipi poles), and dead wood (firewood). Unlike any other Sitka-spruce forest that I had experienced, it was light and airy with a wide range of habitats and wildlife. A network of paths intersected the woodland and native trees in the old hedgerow banks provided broadleaf corridors for birds. In one corner of the woods the culverts that ran under the access trackway had become blocked and this had led to the formation of a native woodland habitat in which the spruce trees had been unable to tolerate the damp ground and had been overtaken by the native willows and alders. One day, in an uncharacteristic act of anarchy, I blocked up one of the culverts in an attempt to encourage the native woodland ecosystem. Over several days I watched as the trackway flooded and a marshy area spread across the forest floor. I had initiated some kind of ecological process and I observed with fascination and awe at the large impact generated from such a small act. Shortly after my vigilante act I returned from one of my forays in the 'little forest' (as it was known) to find the floor of my home sodden with a shallow trickle of water running through it. On investigation I discovered that a ditch on the wooded hillside above my pitch had become blocked and the watercourse had diverted itself through my tent. At first I couldn't quite believe the co-incidence, and looked for signs of sabotage. The blockage appeared, however, to have been the result of years of gradual silting up.

~

July 1996, Village field, Tipi Valley

It was very late and the moon was high as I wound my way home after a thumping folk-music session at the local pub. My head was swimming and my stomach queasy. I was longing for my bed by the time I stumbled into the village fields, only to find another party past its best. A small crowd of whisky-fuelled revellers cheered on the two drunken figures on horseback. They were both holding reins in one hand and a tipi pole each in the other. I wondered what on earth was going on. The two riders were trying to guide their horses away from each other. The horses were giving them a hard time. Then I realised. Jousting! The two riders were attempting to position themselves for a charge. I watched bemused for a moment and then the pounding in my head made my decision for me. One party was enough for me. I staggered home.

~

August 1996, Lawrenny, Pembrokeshire

The shrill sound of the bagpipes forced me awake. As the familiar crown of tipi poles above me came into focus, it took me a moment to orientate myself. "Where am I? What is that bloody noise so damned early in the morning?" My head was musty from the previous night's drumming revelry. Then I remembered; I was at 'Dance Camp Wales'. I leant out of bed and pulled up the fringe of my tipi cover to see who was making that infernal racket. Out in the field before me, in a clearing surrounded by nylon tents the band 'Rasalila' was playing East-European folk music for the early morning circle dancers. I heard Irish Steve next door swearing. I smiled to myself and remembered: it had been a good night.

~

8th January 1997, Triangle field, Tipi Valley

The tension in the air was palpable. The sounds of her labour, which had haunted us all through the previous night, had a new urgency to them. The whole village was waiting. Laurie's lodge had become the centre of a hive of industry for a handful of women. The rest of the tribe kept a respectful low profile whilst she was giving birth. At irregular intervals through the night her primal shouts had echoed across the village. Tents are not very soundproof. Tipi births were common, and the village midwifes were very experienced, though the length of time which she had been in labour was beginning to become a concern. For thirty-six hours Laurie had been having contractions. A pause in the sound. A long silence. And then the sweet sound of the conch (horn) sailed through the valley bringing the news. Relief flowed through the village. A new baby had been born. All was well in the tribe.

~

I had long been aware that many of the tipi people seemed to harbour a glint of the wild in their eyes. At first I had thought that this stemmed from living as outlaws. In time I came to understand that this fiery ember had its origins in the land itself. It was in fact rooted in people's relationships with wilderness. Living under canvas had brought me into direct contact with wild nature. At night I could hear the polecats, hedgehogs and toads. Occasionally they would come into the lodge to explore. To make peace with the wild nature outside I had to make peace with the wild nature inside. I uncovered an inner fire which was both empowering and humbling. It instilled in me a deep respect for the natural order of things.

Tipi Valley had achieved, to my mind, something incredible. It had re-forged the link between human-beings and the Earth. A link that is second nature amongst native people. Whilst some of the methods were challenging from a mainstream perspective, it had actually succeeded in achieving its primary goal.

In establishing my life in Tipi Valley, I found myself part of an entirely different culture. The transition had involved adopting a completely new Earth-based lifestyle, assimilating new codes of conduct and embracing new philosophies. Even the language in Tipi Valley had incorporated so much unique slang that it verged on being a local dialect. Smoking marijuana was a fairly prominent part of Tipi Valley culture. I had found smoking 'grass' (as it was known) very liberating at first, encouraging me to rejoice in the present moment and opening doors of perception to some of the subtler realms. After time, however, I chose to move away from it, preferring a clarity of consciousness that supported independent cognitive thinking.

It took me several years to fully understand the social structures and hierarchies that operated at Tipi Valley, being largely discreet and informal in their nature. It was a cross between tribal culture and anarchy. For the most part it worked very well. In time, though, certain events and attitudes began to unsettle me. Due to the lack of any common forum through which controversies could be considered, there was a trend toward rules and traditions only being enforced when the enforcers considered it appropriate. In effect, a form of strong-arm politics ruled the place, and there was seemingly no accountability as to how this might be applied. The shadow aspects of life in tipi valley had begun to unravel for me.

~

June 1997, Village field, Tipi Valley

The Big-lodge was still on its winter pitch and had been in a sorry state for some months. There had been another attempt to rally the people into moving it up the hill and I had come down to the village fields to help. I had taken the Big-lodge cover down. It would need two people to wheel-barrow it uphill to the winter pitch; one pulling and one pushing. Having taken up two poles already I estimated there were about sixteen more trips to be made. I had approached a few other folk who were all too busy to get involved. I felt sad that such a great tribe could not even come together to coordinate such a simple task. I resolved to carry one more pole and then walk way.

~

Whilst I had whole-heartedly embraced the tipi lifestyle, over time I became aware of the limitations of life under canvas. During my latter years at the valley there was already a move towards yurts (a traditional Mongolian tent) as an alternative to tipis. They had the advantages of being brighter inside, having more headspace and cleaner air (yurts generally used woodburners rather than open fires). For my part, particularly having spent three years studying architecture, I longed to build something more permanent using locally sourced materials, rather than canvas made from imported cotton impregnated with water retardant chemicals. This, along with a desire to explore a more structured approach to both social organisation and land management, led me to begin touring and exploring other settlements and communities in the area. Jeni and I had recently gone our separate ways and this added impetus to my desire to move on. I felt particularly drawn to one project over in North Pembrokeshire.

Chapter 2
Brithdir Mawr; Working together

It was difficult to leave the tribe. Indeed I am not sure that in my heart I ever really did. I needed to take some time and consider where I might go and what I might do next. I wanted to learn. I wanted to grow.

I travelled to India and spent six months travelling from the Himalayas in the north-west to the plains of Bihar in the north-east. I delighted in the joy and faith of the people there and studied the various spiritual paths that form the foundations of their culture. It was a time for cleansing and reflection for me. I returned to the UK revitalised and ready to embark on my next venture.

Brithdir Mawr was an intentional farming community set in the beautiful Pembrokeshire Coast National Park at the foot of the enigmatic 'Carn Ingli' (Welsh for 'Mountain of Angels'). The 165 acres of mixed pasture and woodland held a particular pristine resonance, having never been worked as an agri-business. The network of small fields, green lanes and woodland retained a sense of having been carefully shaped by human hands. By the time I moved to the project, the neglected farm had been turned around to create the foundation for an alternative community. Most of the farmstead buildings were made from stone and slate and had been rebuilt with an unusual sensitivity to detail. A micro-hydro generator, complemented with a photovoltaic array, had been installed to provide some electricity for the project. I was inspired by the land and its potential as a setting for a land-based community and I was impressed by the dedication of the people living there. To begin with I pitched my yurt in the lower fields. The joining process for the community was thorough, requiring full approval from all community members. After a six month trial period I was formally accepted to live there.

The project had originally been initiated by a visionary couple who had bought the farm and laid the foundations for the community. Julian was a very tall man with a child-like twinkle in his eye and a long grey beard. Emma was a focused woman with a wild frizz of hair. They had befriended the local people and were on good terms with all of the neighbours. This was a welcome change from Tipi Valley, where I felt we were generally regarded with suspicion by local people. They had invited carefully selected friends to join them in manifesting their vision of a spiritually motivated group of people working the land together. It was a fully intentional community in which the members, whilst having their own private residences, shared their lives to quite a high degree. It took courage to open and commit to the project, and for me it was the power of the vision that enabled this to happen. In some ways moving there felt rather like adopting a new extended family.

'The whole is greater than the sum of the parts' is one observation on community life, and it was certainly true at Brithdir Mawr. The dozen or so adults and accompanying children, all good people in their own right, shared community workdays, communal meals and meetings. In many ways this structured approach to working together was just what I had been yearning for in my latter years at Tipi Valley. Working the farm as a team was a very efficient approach to time management and was lots of fun at times. Land based tasks are often slow and laborious, especially when you adopt a traditional approach. We would coppice the woodland using axes and two-handed saws to harvest a fuel supply for the community. Cutting firewood on your own can feel overwhelming. Coppicing in a traditional way with a large group of people feels effective, rewarding and inspiring.

~

December 1998, Alder coppice area, Brithdir Mawr

The cold mist closed in around the woodcutters. The sound of axes and saws resounded on and on. There were three teams of people working at a short distance from each other. In and around the branches of a fallen alder tree one group was trimming back the twigs using loppers and bowsaws. The cut twigs were being stacked in different piles according to their thickness. In another place a pair of workers were cutting a freshly fallen tree trunk into sections with a double handed saw. The long blade glided back and forth through the deepening cut, the careful rhythm sending showers of small wood-chippings towards the ground. Concentration showed on the cutters' faces as they focused on the harmonious movement required. A little further away Tone and Emma, knee deep in mud, were working with axes, taking it in turns to cut a wedge from the large alder trunk. Julian stood at some distance taking the strain on a long rope which was attached high up in the tree. Felling a tree of this size was a slow process involving careful calculation and coordination to control its fall. Nearby was last-years coppice area, already six foot high in new growth where the stumps had sprouted in profusion. I put the tray of tea, coffee and cake down onto the wet grass and hollered "Tea's up!" Slowly the noises of industry ceased and the people gathered to warm their hands on the hot drinks.

~

Sharing communal meals was undoubtedly a very efficient use of human and material resources. Food was largely grown on the farm and the meals were wholly nourishing. I have very fond memories of parsnip curries, fruit puddings and home-made wines. We would take it in turns to cook for the community and it was a great way of experiencing a varied diet. I would cook about once a fortnight and it would take me most of the day to conjure a feast. If someone was not inclined to be social on a particular evening then they could collect some food and eat at home. This option worked particularly well for families with young children.

The children in the community did not go to school. They attended tutored lessons at home two mornings a week until they were about fourteen, when they attended the local college. It was a system that, due to the skills of the parents in listening and responding to their childrens' needs, worked incredibly well. The home-educated adolescents seemed mature and self-aware to a degree that far surpassed their peers in mainstream education.

One of the farm outbuildings had been converted into a three-bedroomed hostel. Thus we were able to offer visitors the opportunity to stay in return for a small fee.

Some people would visit and keep themselves to themselves; others would get wholly involved in the project. In addition we would occasionally take on long-term volunteers. These temporary residents played a very important role energetically, bringing fresh ideas and perspectives to the project.

Tony Wrench (Tone), a giant bear of a man, had been invited to live at Brithdir Mawr with his partner Jane Faith in the early days of the community. He was given the opportunity to build a low-impact house, something which he had been dreaming about for some time. He wanted to show that it was possible to build a low-impact worker's cottage from natural local materials, which cost very little money and provided a well-designed home. Tone excavated a south-facing bank and put up a circular timber frame structure sufficient to carry the turf roof. The roof was insulated using straw bales, and the walls were built using cordwood. It was a very simple and practical house, which quickly blended into the landscape.

~

1st February 1999, Carn Ingli

Imbolc. Led by drum and flute, our procession wound its way up the mountain to the spring. The low winter sunshine shone weakly. We stepped carefully through gorse, reed, moss and heather, towards the source. Where once the spring had issued freely onto the mountain, it was now housed in a small brick chamber which fed a pipe and, in turn, our community. The lid was carefully removed and our group held hands and sang blessings upon the spring. A ceremony of thanks for the water. Beautiful songs with harmonies. The mountain received them with warmth. Offerings of flowers and cakes were left. The lid replaced, we began to weave our way back down the mountain. For me the ritual nurtured a sense of humility and gratitude for our place in the web of life.

~

March 1999, Upper hay field, Brithdir Mawr

I took a few steps into the field and turned back to admire the work. Behind me lay some fifty metres of newly laid hedge glistening in the mist. Where there had once been a straggly overgrown hedgerow line there was now a thick, stock-proof hedge. Piles of logs and twigs had been neatly stacked a short distance into the field. I was wet through. My woollen clothes had reached saturation. My hands were sore from wet leather gloves and hawthorn scratches. My heart was glowing. "That should see you through to next winter" I said to the hedge. Feeling proud, I picked up my billhook and bowsaw and headed off to make a drink of hot chocolate.

~

May 1999, Lower hay field, Brithdir Mawr

"I am of the minerals, I am of the plants
I am of the animals, I am of the dance,
I am of the dance...."

I was one of a small group of people singing. Harmonies upon harmonies wove into our beautiful surroundings. A Beltane fire burned brightly in our midst. I could sense the ancestors standing at a distance and observing the event with warm approval. The stars shone brightly.

~

Like Tipi Valley, the community at Brithdir Mawr underwent a spiritual cleansing every full moon with a sweatlodge. This was essentially a ritualised sauna. The Native-American sweatlodge tradition has been passed down from generation to generation and its lineage remains unbroken. The Celtic spiritual traditions, on the other hand, have been largely forgotten over the last two millennia. The sweatlodge ceremony offers the opportunity for a more direct communication with the world of spirit. Whilst this form of prayer was not everyone's cup of tea, it served as a rhythmic meeting point for the community. It was certainly a very powerful tool in my own inner journey, connecting me to the spirits of the land.

After living in the community for about a year Emma and I became partners. She was a very intuitive person with a strong affinity for the spirit world. Her familiarity with the etheric realms was an inspiration to me, and encouraged me to open deeper to the world of God, spirit guides and devas. At the time she was mostly living in her own small, hidden roundhouse in the woods. For three years we lived a very simple lifestyle, seeking a balance point between our own inner natures and the natural world around us. We grew skilled at the traditional crafts of land management and animal husbandry. We specialised in training horses for fieldwork and timber haulage, and this work I found deeply rewarding on many levels. It is a tremendous feeling to long-rein a team of horses pulling a ton weight and there is something very ancient about human and horse uniting in intent to work together. Above all, however, they became dear friends, teaching me a lot about my own human nature.

~

July 2000, Goat field, Brithdir Mawr

At last we were ready. Domino, our fifteen-hand piebald mare, stood before me in full working harness. From the huge elliptical collar around her neck, two chains led behind her to the wooden 'swindle tree'. This was sitting on the ground beside the chain harrow. "Staaandiing", I commanded as I leant down to shackle the swindle tree to the harrow. This was always a slightly tense moment, for were she to walk on or make any sudden move, I would probably be knocked off my feet and injured. My senses were fully attuned to her. Her ears and stance indicated that she was fully attuned to me. We both knew what was coming. With an abrupt swing of her head she let me know that she did not like the chain harrow. Nonetheless, with steadfast obedience she stood still for me, trust and patience personified. We were ready. I moved into position. "Waaalk on", I commanded. She took a deep sigh, and then leant forward and took the strain. The harrow sprang to life with a clanking rumble. I stood still as she walked on, until I was happy with the length of rein between us. Falling in behind her I steered towards the top of the field where the thick bracken had grown to dominate the area. Our task was to crush the growing bracken in order to clear the field for grazing. As we reached the young growth I clicked twice to indicate it was time for us to pick up pace. Full concentration from both of us. Domino listened intently to my every sound, I watched every move she made. The clattering roar of the harrow surrounded us. The sweet smell of horse-sweat, leather and crushed bracken enveloped us. Man and horse working in harmony.

~

Whenever we needed help with the horses we would draw upon the expertise of Geraint, a local Welshman who had worked with horses all of his life. He helped us to understand both the nature of the horses and the technicalities involved in developing a good working relationship with them. We often met up at Llanybydder horse fair, where I could observe the full spectrum of the human-equine relationship. It was an event that was a timeless fusion of traditional farmers, gypsies, pony riders, thoroughbred breeders and horse-meat traders. For horses it was an extremely stressful experience; to be confined within a small stall in close proximity to many other unfamiliar horses. They were examined by people of all ilk, and then paraded in front of crowds and auctioned off to the highest bidder. I witnessed the many approaches that people have adapted to the art of mastering horses, from the outright abusive to the gentle horse whisperers. It also provided a rare opportunity for us to purchase traditional working harness, which was generally regarded as the redundant remnants of a bygone era.

~

28th July 2000, Gelli, South Pembrokeshire

We were on our way to Dance Camp Wales. Night was closing in as we approached a spot we had identified on the map as having good possibilities as a place to spend the night. Domino was tired from fifteen miles of pulling our home-made barrel-top cart. In general people were delighted when they saw us on the road and it was not uncommon to be asked for photographs. However we were often met with opposition when seeking a place to stop overnight and rest. The place we had chosen was a pretty picnic area by a stream, and as we pulled over we noted a fluttering curtain in the nearby cottage. We set to work quickly to settle ourselves in and within fifteen minutes Domino had been brushed down, fed and tethered and our dinner was cooking on a small fire. Sure enough, we were then visited by a man with some authority over the field. "What do you think you're doing? Don't you know this is private property!" he demanded. Fortunately, after some persuasion, he was amenable to us staying one night, so long as we were gone by nine'o'clock the following morning. We relaxed and enjoyed the rest of the evening with home-made ginger cake, a little wine and some music.

~

September 2000, Farmhouse pantry, Brithdir Mawr

Still half asleep, I strained the fresh goats' milk from the milking bucket through the muslin cloth and into the enamel jug. I then poured myself half a cup of the frothy liquid for a morning treat. There is nothing quite like fresh goats milk, still warm. It brought my senses into my body a little, helping me in the transition from sleepwalking to woken consciousness. Still in my familiar routine, I placed the enamel jug onto the slate slab next to the bottled gooseberries and blackcurrants, and took what remained from the previous evening's milking over to the cheese-making area. A range of soft cheeses, fetas and cheddars lined the wall. I poured the old milk into the cheese bucket. Picking up a small brown loaf on the way out, I left the dim pantry with bread and milk to return home for breakfast.

~

September 2000, Top middle field, Brithdir Mawr

We leant upon the newly installed cleft-oak gate and considered our work. The line of fence-posts was approximately 150 yards long and, along with the gateway, now created a sturdy stock-proof barrier between the 'middle field' and the 'oak grove field'. Nobody but us, however, would really know the work that had gone into this. Six months ago we had begun by selecting a tall oak with a 24inch diameter trunk to fell. Using only axes and saws, two of us had laboured to chop, saw and heave the timber into suitable lengths for the horses to remove from the steep wooded slope. We had then cleaved and shaped the timbers using

froes, hammers and wedges, before selecting the best timbers for the gate. These were then finished with a draw knife, and jointed using pegged mortise and tenon joints. The fence posts were pointed and charred in the fire before being taken to the field for hammering in. On the one hand we felt immense pride in what we had achieved. On the other hand we were astonished at just how much work it had been to create a fence.
"You know, Tone, it makes me really appreciate how much work it must have been for our ancestors to carve out these fields from wilderness."
"No kidding, I'm bloody knackered!"
"Me too!"
We stood in silence, letting the gate support our bodies.

~

In time I built my dream house, hidden away in the woods. It took me a year to complete from beginning to end, working on it one day a week. I began by selecting ash trees from the woodland, whose trunks would make good posts, beams and rafters, and then cut and carried them to the site. I then stripped off the bark and jointed them together to build a circular wood-henge frame with a reciprocating rafter roof. Onto this conical roof I tied a spiral of hazel rods. A sewn calico sheet then separated nine inches of straw insulation from the butyl rubber membrane onto which sat the turf. A floor made from rough-sawn planks was then attached to the posts and a straw bale wall, along with various second-hand double glazed units, was built around the posts. I constructed one opening window opposite the doorway to allow air flow through the hut. The door itself was canvas lined with blankets. Into one wall I built an open fire which served as both a heating and a cooking source combined. The house cost £900 to build and was beautiful, dry, light, and very cosy.

As a community we kept quiet about the roundhouses (along with a series of other developments which had occurred without planning consent). This we did in full knowledge of the potential planning scandal that could occur, and with good reason, as without doubt we would have been refused planning permission had we applied ahead of time. One day, Tone's roundhouse was spotted by a pilot flying a small aeroplane overhead. Apparently he saw sunlight reflecting off a solar panel on the roof. The heavy hammer of the planning system then fell on Brithdir Mawr.

In all there were seventeen planning violations, though many were very minor. Most elements we were able to resolve, including a timber dome dwellinghouse that had been built in one of the gardens. This was granted a 'certificate of lawful use' by virtue of having been occupied for longer than four years. Some elements remained hidden in the woods (such as my roundhouse). Tone's roundhouse became a big planning issue.

Tone went on to fight an epic campaign with the planners over his roundhouse. Taking on the planning system is not for the faint-hearted, and the tiresome bureaucratic wrangle that ensued was an enormous emotional strain, sometimes manifesting in physical illness. Tone's media-friendly approach, however, was very effective in bringing awareness to low-impact development. He embarked on a sharp learning curve in information technology and spearheaded his campaign with a website. His roundhouse appeared in every national newspaper and on many television channels, and became an icon for the legitimisation of low-impact development.

~

10th November 2000, Planning Inspectorate Public Enquiry, Newport Memorial Hall

We filed out of the stuffy hall to be greeted by sweet fresh air. We had mixed feelings of hope and despair. I was exhausted after having spent many days helping Tone prepare and deliver his appeal to the Planning Inspector. Our barrister looked drained – she had been incredible to watch, and I suspect the diet of strong coffee and tobacco was taking its toll. We had given it our best shot. We had certainly given the planners a run for their money. Would it be good enough? Time would tell. For the moment we were content to allow our busy minds to settle and once again feel the sky above our heads and the earth beneath our feet.

~

25th January 2001, Farmhouse kitchen, Brithdir Mawr

"I find... that the retention of the appeal dwelling would have a harmful effect on the natural beauty of its national park surroundings." We sat in disbelief as the Inspector's report was read out. The report went on to say that Tone's house was to be demolished within 18 months. I felt saddened and frustrated at society's

inability to change. What was it going to take before people could live lightly on the Earth? How many environmental disasters must be witnessed before alternative solutions would be permitted? If the situation were not so grave it would seem ridiculous. The faces around the table were downcast.

~

Alongside our planning issues other challenges began to manifest in the community.

As part of our move towards self-reliance we erected a wind turbine to boost our electrical production capability. We were aiming to be independent of mains electricity. The turbine was mounted on a ten metre mast held in place with a series of steel ties anchored to the ground. Periodically the turbine would need maintenance or repair and this required the turbine and mast to be lowered to the ground for access. On one such occasion a television crew, attracted by the controversy surrounding Tone's roundhouse, was present. Midway through the turbine's descent the cameraman ran underneath so that he might get a better angle, the turbine fell and crashed onto him. He was very seriously injured. One moment's oversight had led to a man becoming permanently disabled. It was a wake-up call as to the importance of health and safety. Liability claims and legal actions followed. After this incident it became very difficult for the community to renew its insurance, which in turn led to the hostel being forced to close. This was a massive loss for the project because the hostel was the primary route through which visitors passed through the project.

Decisions in the community were taken by consensus. This meant that any change would need the approval of everybody. Many traditional native cultures make decisions by consensus, and in many ways this seems to me the wisest approach. A consensus decision within a circle creates a powerful impulse to the universe, and cultivates a sense of common purpose. It does however run the risk of progress being blocked by a minority. At times I did witness this happen in the community and it led to confusion and stagnation, both of which were damaging to the spirit of the project.

In order to foster a culture of goodwill amongst the people, it felt important for all community members to be equitably contributing to the whole. Yet people found themselves with different needs and possibilities in the different phases of their lives. For example, families with young children, or illness, have different levels of time and energy to give to the wider community than young single adults. People also have varied skills, talents and approaches to offer. Therefore community contributions took different forms; from cooking to gardening, from childcare to financial income. We didn't always agree about the value of these various contributions. It was sometimes a challenge to find a balance so that all the members felt good about their respective inputs. There were also times in which the community was supporting a person or household. Resentments arose easily and were difficult to dispel.

Whilst we had created a structure in which most of our physical needs were met through the community, we struggled to balance the emotional and social needs of the people. Intentional community life needs diligent personal management as well as good practical management to work smoothly. Thus in addition to the weekly business meetings, we created a forum to share feelings at a weekly sharing meeting. Much was resolved, but sometimes the undercurrents ran too deep. Community life began to get intense and political.

One of the issues that arose stemmed from the nature of the built forms. Some of us had moved onto the land, effectively creating a new infrastructure. Others remained in the old farmhouse and outbuildings. It was apparent that the labour needed to service the traditional infrastructure was far in excess of the labour required to service the new, more sustainable infrastructure. The farmhouse and outbuildings were built at a time when there was a cheap and plentiful supply of both coal and labour. These old dwellings were built with massive stone walls, numerous fireplaces and no insulation. In renovating the farmhouse and resolving to heat it with firewood, we had in effect created a system which required a very demanding workload. Our new roundhouses on the other hand were very well insulated and designed for occupants who could live lightly on the Earth. Frustrated with the planning limitations upon us we dreamed of creating a new ecovillage where a sustainable infrastructure could be implemented from the outset. Tired of the community politics, we dreamed of a more liberal community structure in which people held equal power and were free to live independently.

In addition to the core issue of distributing the workload fairly, other structural challenges arose.

Brithdir Mawr was undergoing the very necessary transformation from benevolent dictatorship to independent community. This involved a shift in power and responsibility that required deep trust on both sides. A trust that, when it came to it, wavered.

Whilst an inspiring vision for the project had been well expressed, particularly by Emma, the project founders had deliberately held back from writing down or defining this vision; wanting this final declaration to come from the group itself. The vision revolved around a community of people working the land together for the common good. They were both clear that when the group had reached a point of being able to take responsibility for the project, then the farm's ownership would be transferred to a Trust. When the group itself felt it was ready for this shift and were keen, as a part of this process, to define the vision, we were met with doubt and delay from the founders. Many of us began to feel frustrated at the seeming unwillingness for the handover of ownership to happen. I personally felt as if I had committed years of my life to a promise that was not being honoured. It was a tumultuous time in which the very foundations of the project seemed to be shifting. It became clear that in the interim period between the project's inception, and it reaching a point where the group felt it was ready to become independent, the two founders' visions had diverged to the point of incompatibility. Emma's vision had become increasingly mystical, focusing on creating a group committed wholly to raising consciousness and bringing about spiritual awakening. Julian had become alarmed at some of the uncompromising attitudes being expressed, and had begun to doubt his own position within the project. As a group we found ourselves in a position of conflict and we did what we could to find resolution. However the real power lay with the legal owners, and as such our consensus decision-making circle was redundant and it was in the hands of Emma and Julian to find a solution.

This impasse was eventually resolved by the project being effectively split into two, and the two founders retaining control over their respective halves. Naturally I continued living in the woods with Emma, a lifestyle with which I was very content.

~

Summer Solstice 2001, Carn Ingli

The rising sun pierced the misty cloud for just a moment, banishing the remnants of night and heralding the new day. Scattered around the mountain's peak, various groups of watchers whooped and cheered the shining golden light of dawn. Some had sat vigil through the night, others had risen early to climb to the summit. All had come to honour the Earth in their own way.

~

Mid-July 2001, The hay fields, Brithdir Mawr

I steered the flat-bed cart past the woodshed and into the hay field. The ash branches by the gateway scraped the side of the cart and I realised that I had just missed the enormous gateway stone by too narrow a margin for comfort. I needed to rest. We also needed the hay in. Domino pulled with a vigour that matched the tension in the air. Sweat lathered where the harness rubbed her body. I set my course through the field. There were about twenty people working there; either stacking the hay bales into piles or loading trailers pulled by tractor, horse and car. The sense of a community pulling together was exhilarating. The grey clouds overhead loomed ominously. I was exhausted from four days of haymaking. This year we had managed to cut about half an acre with the horses using an ancient horse-drawn finger-mower that we had recently purchased and renovated. The horses had hated the noise and vibration of it and it was clear that we needed to do a lot of work to bring it back to smooth operation. We had cut the remaining twelve or so acres using our old Massey Ferguson tractor. Following that we had been blessed with a run of fine weather and had managed to do most of the turning by horse, repeatedly folding the hay over in the field using a hay-rake, until it became light and fragrant. The choice between horse and tractor was always highlighted at hay-making. The most difficult nut to crack was baling the hay; this was simply not possible to do without a tractor, and past attempts at storing loose hay had not worked well. Throughout the process my hayfever had plagued me. It wouldn't be long before we were finished and then I would go and splash my face with cold water and lie down somewhere cool and dark. In the meantime I stood at Domino's head, taking time to be still and present in the moment, as the cart was loaded with bales.

~

August 2001, Penquoit farm, 'Dance Camp Wales'

It was the early morning circle dance session at 'Dance Camp Wales'. I stood as part of the band, Rasalila, in the centre of the circle of dancers. Playing music required a total presence of mind from me, and was as much about listening as producing any sound. The medieval song was delivered with the power and honour it deserved. Drum, mandola, pipes and fiddle accompanied.

"Cuncti simus concanentes, Ave Maria
Cuncti simus concanentes, Ave Maria
Virgo sola existente, en affuit angelus
Gabriel est appelatus, atque missus caelitus
Clara facieque dixit, Ave Maria
Clara facieque dixit, Ave Maria"

About two dozen dancers whirled in unison as the sun climbed higher. The band and dancers were watched by a scattering of people sitting around on the grass.

~

One of the things that I had wanted to explore with my life at Brithdir Mawr was quite how 'eco' I could be? Could I live without causing any pollution? I had all my own bread, eggs, milk, goats' cheese and vegetables supplied as part of the community as well as a good portion of my fruit and honey. I did purchase butter, tea, pasta, toothpaste, candles, clothes and other odd things like guitar strings and chocolate covered brazil-nuts. I could never get completely away from producing some plastic waste, albeit a carrier-bag full a month. I travelled wherever I could by horse, though sometimes I did use cars and trains to visit family or for gigs with the band. Occasionally I would still visit libraries, doctors, cafes and cinemas, and all these activities had an ecological impact. If I wanted to be a part of society in any way I was going to have to accept that there was going to be some compromise. I already felt as if I existed on the outer fringes of society, my life having more in common with that of a medieval peasant rather than anything from the 21st century.

~

April 2002, Newport High Street

"Well, aren't you going to tidy that up?" the lady asked sternly. I looked down in confusion at where she pointed, as a light scattering of loose hay shifted about in the breeze. "This is private property you know!" she continued haughtily. Domino shifted uneasily and indicated her irritation with the lady's tone of voice. The lady, clearly unnerved by the sheer size of Domino, gave a huff of disapproval and marched off down the street. "Well then girl," I gently whispered to Domino, reassuring her with my tone of voice that all was well, "looks like we're in trouble again." Domino let out a deep sigh. I loaded the pack-bags onto her back and considered how best to deal with the offending remnants of hay that Domino had left. I gathered up a fistful and put it in my pocket, then swept the remnants away with my feet, letting the wind catch them and carry them down the road. I was acutely aware that we were being discreetly watched by a few of the townsfolk. I felt saddened at the lack of compassion and

understanding for what I was trying to do. It seemed that it was not possible in today's world to find a safe place to tie up a horse whilst I went shopping. "At least you didn't do a poo this time!" I joked with Domino before untying her lead-rope from the railing and leading her away up the street. The sound of her shod feet echoed loudly off the shop-fronts and houses.

~

May 2002, my round-house, Brithdir Mawr

I reached a place of total satisfaction and contentment with my life. I had everything I had dreamed of; a natural house in a beautiful setting, land-based work that I loved, music and celebration, community. I was very happy. I had developed an intimate relationship with God and gratitude turned to surrender. I offered my life in service to God. And God welcomes all things.

~

June 2002, my round-house, Brithdir Mawr

Darkness. Deeper and deeper I fell into the void. Submerging ever deeper into the lowest of frequencies. Through fear, through panic, through absolute terror; into the velvet depths. Surrender. Heartfelt surrender. For days and days I fell, with a smouldering fire and my drum to guide me. My belly churning, heaving and unravelling. When I tuned into my thoughts, they were full of panic and terror at what I was experiencing. So I stayed focused on my heart. It had become my anchor and my light. It was all I could do. Somewhere deep inside I was aware that I was in some kind of process of surrendering my spirit in service.

I felt a presence beside me, comforting and holding me. "What shall I do?" I asked.... "Its time to leave"... "Where must I go?".... "Follow your heart" ... "Who are you?".... "I am your spirit guide. I am here to help you".... "How can I trust that you are real?".... "My name is Giovanni. You will see that I am real."

A few days later I picked up a book that caught my eye in the farmhouse and opened a page at random to read about a man who lived a long time ago called Giovanni. He was a spiritual seeker.

~

In conventional terms my experience might have been described as a breakdown, or perhaps even schizophrenia. From my perspective it was a breakthrough.

I gave away almost everything that I owned and prepared to leave Brithdir Mawr. I found the process absolutely heart-wrenching. I had developed such a deep love for the land there. I felt very open and vulnerable, occasionally wondering if I had gone mad. My heart, however, was radiant and I was experiencing an incredible connection with the world of spirit that inspired a deep conviction in what I was doing. Saying goodbye to the horses was especially difficult. At first I thought that I would go to America and meet with the Native American Indians, having long felt a kinship with these people. I bought a one-way boat ticket to New York and began to arrange connections there.

In a last minute attempt to raise some funds for the journey I went once again to 'Dance Camp Wales' as a musician. Despite every effort on my part to resist I fell head over heels in love with a beautiful woman called Hoppi. She was a fiery, powerful spirit with a passion for creativity. Within a fortnight my life had turned upside down and I found myself living in a small village in the Sierra Nevada Mountains in Spain. I had only spent three days with her before I knew that I was going to ask her to marry me. I thought it prudent to wait a little, so I asked her a week later.

Chapter 3
Holtsfield; Chalet Oasis

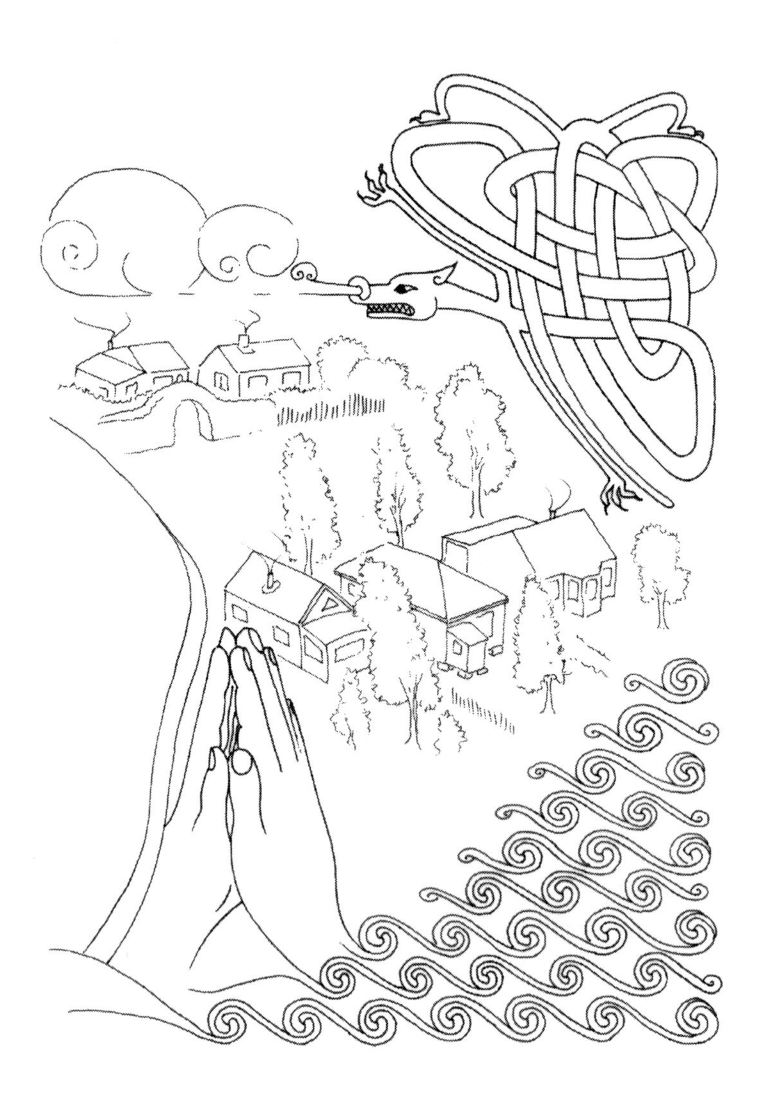

The Spanish culture proved too big a gap for us to bridge and so after some months we headed back to our homeland and set about looking for a family home. Hoppi had one son from a previous partner, Jarro who was two and a half years old. My son, Jarvis, who was thirteen years old by this time, had indicated that he wanted to come and live with me full time. We welcomed him into our home. Hoppi fell pregnant. It seemed that my life had transformed overnight from that of a single man to being part of a family of five.

~

January 10th 2003, Oxwich Bay sand dunes, Gower

Joy of joys. To be married to the woman I love. Stood with my new wife in the middle of a huge circle of friends and family on a sunny January morning. Blessed in our marriage ceremony by Rik the Vic from Tipi Valley. Watched by the sun and the moon. Dressed in our best home-made finery. We sang:

"May my heart reflect your light Lord
As the moon reflects the light of the sun in love,
Always in love
Hu-Allah, Allah-hu Allah, Allah-hu Allah, Allah-hu"

~

We scouted around the UK looking for somewhere to settle. One opportunity sang clearly to us above all others, and so we returned to West Wales and set about trying to rent a vacant chalet on the Gower Peninsular, in a place called Holtsfield.

Holtsfield was sited about half a mile inland from the Gower coast, next to the Bishopswood Nature Reserve, a secluded wooded valley featuring oak, ash and beech. There were 27 chalets there: a funky collection of lightweight shacks ranging from ramshackle to derelict. They were all unique and somewhat endearing due to their human scale and unorthodox construction. The main gathering point for the community was a large picnic table next to a dilapidated notice board. These sat in the village green around which the chalets were clustered. The site had seen very little development over recent years and mature trees had grown up throughout the settlement creating a forest glade impression.

Holtsfield was owned by an infamous local solicitor called Mr Jones. Due to a long-standing legal stalemate between him and the residents, the chalets had been held in a kind of economic bubble over the previous two decades. Most of the residents either paid little or no rent at all, and the properties themselves, by virtue of their legal status, remained unaffected by the ever rising values placed on the conventional housing market. This was undoubtedly a key factor in the somewhat leisurely pace of life there. In my experience people unencumbered by heavy financial overheads generally slow down and enjoy life a bit more. In some ways it reminded me of a shanty-town; if repairs were made on chalets they tended to be made with recycled or reclaimed materials. That was part of its charm.

People resided there under various different legal arrangements. The secure tenants had won the legal right to live there, though Mr Jones was refusing to acknowledge this right and would not accept rent from them. Others had no legal rights and were squatting, occasionally receiving threatening eviction notices from the landlord. In recent years a new category of residency had been created, and this was where our opportunity lay; Mr Jones had begun to let some of the empty chalets using 6 month rolling tenancies. To enter into such a contract was an initiation in itself.

~

February 2003, Solicitor's Office, Swansea

Mr Jones' secretary kept us waiting for the best part of an hour in the gloomy cluttered reception stacked floor to ceiling with towers of dusty boxes and files. When at last he agreed to see us, we entered a room dominated by the most enormous desk I have ever seen, buried in piles of paper. Pictures of the Welsh rugby team hung on walls decorated with faded wallpaper. We picked our way carefully over the boxes to two chairs, to face the formidable Welshman through a cloud of cigarette smoke. He was a large bearded man with a stern expression. He addressed us in a weary, nonchalant manner. He spoke with bitterness about the Holtsfield situation and how he had been unjustly treated. He spoke about the intimidation that he and his family had experienced and it was clear that he harboured deep resentment at what had happened. The conversation changed tack. He asked us whether we were on the run or wanted by the authorities. "No" we replied indignantly. He went on to question us about Welsh politics and rugby. He was a very intelligent, somewhat cynical man who warmed to our naivety. After some time discussing the Holtsfield situation his attitude shifted and he adopted a fatherly manner towards us. He indicated that he was willing to deal with us, much to our relief.

~

March 2003, 22 Holtsfield

Having had a good look at the chalet from the outside, we furtively climbed in through the bathroom window to have a closer look at what we were considering taking on. The house had clearly been empty for some time. It was gloomy and absolutely filthy. The floor in one corner of the bathroom had collapsed where the roof had been leaking. We moved cautiously into the kitchen. It appeared as if the place had been abandoned in haste. There was a basin of foul greasy water in the kitchen sink. I tipped it down the plug-hole only to watch it splash onto the floor beneath. Meanwhile Hoppi had opened the door of one of the fridges to find that it was full of green hairy meat. The stench had become overwhelming and we both made a dash for the window, Hoppi retching, both of us gasping for some fresh air. Whilst I felt repulsion at the layer of filth I could appreciate the structure beneath. It was something I could work with.

~

Despite his reputation, our landlord proved to be fair and considerate with us, even donating a washing machine. The chalet that we agreed to rent was in need of substantial works and we agreed to do this in lieu of twelve months rent. Sections of the roof were missing and one of the walls swayed alarmingly in the wind. The building was infested with rats and dry rot had taken hold of one corner of the chalet. The garden was a tangle of overgrown privet, brambles and young ash trees. We set ourselves to the task in hand and worked like dogs for ten weeks. I did all the building and carpentry work and Hoppi did the plumbing and electrics. This became increasingly difficult for her as she neared the end of her pregnancy. This was not through any lull in her energy but rather was more down to the logistical challenge of getting into the corners and tight spaces where services tend to accumulate. Friends helped us from time to time and we were very grateful for this. We rebuilt the chalet on a budget of £2500, recycling everything that we could, and created a beautiful home. The morning after we had finished painting and cleaning up, Hoppi's waters broke. Throughout the day I moved the bare essentials into our new home and our new neighbours blessed us with gifts of flowers and candles. That evening Hoppi gave birth to our new baby daughter in the chalet. It was an incredible moment that no words can describe. The midwives arrived an hour after the birth, just in time to examine the placenta. They had been sitting in their car at the top of the track waiting for over an hour for a 4x4 to carry them down the rough track.

The underlying social structure at Holtsfield seemed to be close to that of a conventional village model. There were no meetings, no joining procedures and no obligations to contribute to the community in any way. People lived in nuclear families and were as open or closed as they chose to be. Most children attended the local school. Everybody knew everybody and an attitude of acceptance seemed to prevail. It seemed that generally diversity was welcomed without judgement or condemnation. It was a community in the traditional sense of the word. The sense of social liberty was very welcome after my experiences at Brithdir Mawr. It dawned to me that there was much to be said for this conventional village model; it had evolved over many lifetimes with good reason, and allowed for freedom and flexibility.

Our chalet was basically a higgledy-piggledy shed which had been extended, patched and changed dozens of times over many decades. It had been built using 'three by two' inch timbers with the cavities filled with mineral-fibre insulation. The walls were clad in timber and the roof was finished in roofing-felt. Over the years the roof had sagged and the walls bent outwards, giving the roofline a smile and the chalet a lazy appearance. It was very small for a family of five, being only eight metres long and six metres wide (with a tiny upstairs attic). It was heated by a woodburner and ventilated by draughts in every corner. Every window was slightly different in shape and style. One of the great things about it was its flexibility; I could put in a new window in an afternoon using just a saw, a hammer and a few nails.

When we first arrived at the chalet, a flush toilet fed a shallow hole in the garden covered over by a piece of corrugated tin. As well as being foul and smelly, it had filled over the years and was now completely dysfunctional. It was clear that we were going to have to install a new toilet. I was of the opinion that we should install a compost toilet, the likes of which I was familiar with from my time at Brithdir Mawr. It took some persuasion on my part to convince Hoppi to give it a try. I built a very simple twin-chamber composting toilet onto the side of the chalet and she was pleasantly surprised. To filter the grey-water from the house I created a reed-bed system in the garden and planted it with a mix of bulrush, yellow flag and willow. Both systems worked really well, with annual crops of compost, willow withies and mulch for the garden.

Our chalet was very close to the ruins of a small ancient monastery and two holy springs, one of which still flowed freely. Once we had rebuilt the chalet we began collecting drinking water from the spring, rather than drink the mains-supply water which tasted of chlorine. After a series of belly-aches we asked the Environment Agency to test the spring water. They concluded that it was contaminated, probably due to poor sewage management in the area combined with a honeycombed bedrock geology. This saddened me. With reticence we returned to drinking treated water.

For the previous ten years I had lived a semi-reclusive life without electricity, plumbing or central heating. In some ways I found it quite a challenge to return and re-integrate with mainstream consumer society. Part of me resisted the electrical appliances which appeared in our home one by one, but ultimately my surrender to a modern lifestyle was eased by my love for Hoppi, with whom I was blissfully happy. I was also pragmatic; it is one thing to wash your own clothes by hand but to wash a whole family's laundry by hand was simply too laborious and time consuming when there were more pressing issues, like the rent and bills to pay. I was grateful to at least have found a home where an outside fire was a welcome norm and the sound of birdsong prevailed.

For a livelihood, I began with what I could find: building and renovation work in Swansea. Over time I specialised in carpentry. I had some fantastic jobs and really enjoyed opportunities to be creative with wood: such as commissions for beautiful slab-wood desks, a custom staircase and some very picturesque summerhouses. My 'bread and butter' work was repairing and renovating chalets, which I found largely enjoyable once I had got past the stage of removing all the rotten wood, old insulation and rat droppings.

Occasionally I would get work at the Gower Bird Hospital, rebuilding aviaries and animal rehabilitation units. This provided a fascinating insight into the challenges facing local wildlife and again highlighted concerns about biodiversity loss and climate change.

I renovated our garden, maximising on the limited space as best as possible. Working with the steep incline and shade (our garden only received direct sunlight from midday onwards), I created a series of terraces for recreation, food-growing and wildlife.

Our two youngest children were blissfully happy in Holtsfield. The strong sense of community meant that they could play freely. It was common to catch fleeting glimpses of bands of children as they roamed from chalet to chalet, from village green to woods, playing from morning ‘til night.

~

February 2004, 22 Holtsfield

Rhythm is timeless and transcends human consciousness. Each morning I walked over to a neighbouring field to milk our goats. Fresh hay, rolled barley, intimate contact and warm milk. Sensuous, earthy and real. Each evening I returned, to put them away for the night. Wearing a path into the ground between our house and the field. Weaving a rhythm into the ether. Caressing the Earth with a dance. Nourishing both man and Earth beyond the physical.

~

July 2004, Sandy Lane, Gower

The final whistle blew and as my hopes died, I collapsed on the grass. I felt disappointed in myself for having let the Holtsfield football team down. We had been building up to this match for over a month and had really given it our best. However, we were no match for our well-practised opponents. The Sandy-Lane team was avidly celebrating their victory. The supporters and spectators were clapping. My bare chested comrades shook hands with their yellow shirted opponents and dispersed to the sidelines. The Sandy-Lane captain came over to shake my hand. I agreed that it was a good game. “Rematch?” he enquired. “Maybe next year!” I joked, though inside I was not so sure. I reckoned that football was probably not my strength.

~

November 2004, our garden, 22 Holtsfield

It was a dry winter's day. I was sitting in my vegetable garden watching a robin pick at some breadcrumbs that the ducks had left behind. I saw an elderly lady tottering up the footpath with her old collie dog faithfully accompanying her. Moments later I spotted the old lady surreptitiously climbing on the rope swing which I had made for the children. With delight and awe I watched her bravely leap off the tree stump and squeak with delight as she sailed through the air.

~

After a year or so it became clear that we needed to expand our house. Up until that point my teenage son, Jarvis, had been living in the small attic room. With his help I built him a bedroom shed in the garden. The construction was actually much more robust than our chalet. And so he, along with a small crowd of his friends it seemed, moved into the garden. This suited his nocturnal, noisy habits and was a good step forwards for the levels of harmony in our home. It is something that I would recommend for every teenager.

I built a small duck run at the bottom of the garden with a pond for them to swim in and a tall fence to protect them from foxes and stray dogs. During the day they were allowed to wander freely in the small vegetable garden where they sought out slugs and snails. Their passion for slimy creatures made gardening in Wales possible without the use of slug poisons. At night they were put away in a wooden duck house raised high off the ground to protect them from rodents and mink. We had three Khaki Campbells and they provided plenty of eggs for the family. They made a happy little flock and I often saw people walking past on the adjacent footpath enjoying the site of the ducks going about their business.

I also became involved in a horticulture project next door. Ed ran a box-scheme supplying seasonal produce to local people. He had two acres in which he grew a wide range of vegetables. He would deliver by horse drawn cart every Sunday and I would help him out from time to time with either hoeing weeds (which was an epic task on two acres) or horse-work. The opportunity to reconnect with horses was relished by me and on rare occasion I would ride to the beach through the nature reserve simply to remember. I had to be careful doing this though, because the horses were liable to churn up the footpaths with their heavy feet, and many people relied on the network of local paths to get around.

~

February 2005, our garden, 22 Holtsfield

We were sitting around a fire in our back garden. The children were asleep in bed. We sang our prayers to the universe;

"The river is flowing, flowing and growing,

The river is flowing, back to the sea,
Mother Earth carry me, your child I will always be,
Mother Earth carry me, back to the sea."

~

May 2005, our garden, 22 Holtsfield

It was my evening visit to my home-made polytunnel. I found such joy in looking after my tomatoes, cucumbers, lettuce and peppers. In one corner I had built a little stone refuge for the slow-worms that lived here long before me. My cactus also enjoyed the heat that was stored and radiated by the stones. By the door grew a little patch of barley self seeded from a straw mulch I once used. I watered the plants and took time to sit and enjoy the company of my leafy friends.

~

July 2005, 22 Holtsfield

I was sitting on my balcony overlooking the garden in the early evening light. The first stars were beginning to twinkle. The only sound was that of the crickets chirruping. I had rebuilt my life. Where there was a dilapidated shack and a patch of brambles, I had built a home and garden. Where I was once a single man, I was now holding a family. I had wholly re-entered society. I had rent, bills, council tax, a fridge and a washing machine. I had found work, good work which brought in good money. And yet I felt there was more for me to do. "Great spirit, what would you have me do?" ...Silence... And beneath the silence, the sound of the universe unfolding in its own time.

~

The legal situation created a slight feeling of unease in the Holtsfield community. Occasionally rumours would circulate of eviction notices sent from Mr Jones to those who were squatting. For us, there was the task of needing to meet with Mr Jones every six months to renew our tenancy agreement. I recall discussing the prospect of trying to find a community resolution to the legal tangle with various residents there. Each time I considered this it seemed that, even if it were possible to find a unified solution, it simply was not my role as a newcomer in Holtsfield to attempt this. Most of the other chalet settlements on Gower, including Sandy Lane, had managed to buy their own freeholds collectively, and had then proceeded to sell off the individual freeholds to the occupiers. It seemed to me that eventually Holtsfield too would inevitably default to this individual freehold structure. It also seemed that many of the Holtsfielder's would be happy with this as an outcome. Certainly there was no consensus about any alternative legal arrangement. Nonetheless we felt settled in Holtsfield and our new family flourished.

~

9th September 2006, Oxwich Bay, Gower

I was sitting with friends having lunch on a hotel lawn overlooking Oxwich bay. We were surrounded by people in the hustle and bustle of a bank-holiday weekend. Children ran back and forth between the bouncy castle and their drinks on the tables. The sun was out and the weather was fine. I was aware of various streams of conversation around me but my attention wandered off. It was as if a mist descended about me. My focus turned to a dragonfly cruising back and forth. Time slowed. Captivated by its presence and beauty I lost track of the world around me. There was a message there. I listened carefully but try as I might I could not quite discern it. "Papa, papa, come and watch me on the bouncy castle!" my daughter dragged me back to her world.

~

December 2006, Mumbles, Gower

I was standing on the seafront in Mumbles. The tide was in and the sea was calm. I felt the depth of the sea, its massive weight and volume. On some subtle level I felt a deep pulse. I felt it again, like some distant underground boom with a frequency lower than sound. It carried a clear message to me. "The sea will rise. It will breach the coastline. There will be flooding. Change is coming."

~

In Holtsfield the issue of limited service provision was an area of frustration for many people in the community. The entire site was served by a 13mm water pipe and so there were often water shortages in the summer, particularly for those chalets that were higher up. Similarly the rough trackway that led to the community was in terrible condition with a chronic shortage of parking spaces available for residents. There was mixed opinion about upgrading the services. Some people did not want to invest their money in what they saw as the landlord's obligations. Many people did not want to take any action that might encourage additional vehicle use. Holtsfield had been laid out long before the motor car had become so prevalent in our society. In many ways the fact that dwellinghouses were not accessed by roads was part of its charm. As a result of the lack of a consensus regarding upgrading the track or the water pipe, we lived with water shortages in the summer and a crowded bumpy track which took its toll in wear and tear on our cars.

In 2007 Mr Jones began to make moves to settle the legal situation. Those chalets that had been squatted were offered tenancy agreements. Rent was accepted from the secure tenants for the first time, finally honouring their legal rights to live there. Those that had rolling tenancy agreements, like us, and had approached Mr Jones were offered the opportunity to purchase their homes. We welcomed the opportunity to own our home and set about raising the necessary mortgage to do so. It took us the best part of a year to negotiate an agreement with Mr Jones. He was generous to us and I like to think it was because we had not judged him over Holtsfield's history, and instead had approached him without prejudice, developing a relationship of mutual respect. In September 2007 we bought our chalet for a sum which, on the one hand seemed a huge amount of money, and on the other hand was well below the market value: £100,000. All of it was borrowed. We were quite open about our intentions and were surprised when a few of the Holtsfield residents reacted aggressively to us buying our home. It was our direct neighbours who, being the first people to buy, received the lion's share of the aggression in this instance. We were seen to be undermining the community.

One of the shadow aspects of alternative communities and cultures is that of fundamentalism. I had been aware of its influence at Tipi Valley and Brithdir Mawr and had at times participated in and contributed to it. It was not until we came to sell our chalet in Holtsfield that I was given the opportunity to meet it face to face. In the summer of 2008 we decided it was the right time for us to move on from Holtsfield. We planned to sell the chalet and raise funds to help us set up in our next venture. Since our purchase, Mr Jones was in the process of selling off another chalet for £125,000 and was beginning to negotiate further sales in the region of £150,000.

We were aware that our actions would potentially have knock-on effects for those who tried to buy their chalets after us by reinforcing the rising prices of the chalets, and were keen to find ways of keeping this impact down. We invited sealed bids on our chalet from a few friends and were hoping to sell for £150,000; giving us £50,000 to take with us. Whilst we were aware that this would be an incredible deal for us, we reasoned that we had spent about £20,000 in rent over the past 3 years, and spent an additional £10,000 on improvements, and invested a huge amount of time and energy in transforming the place. We were offered that sum from a young Holtsfield couple, though the offer was made with an element of bitterness that made us hold back from agreeing. Other offers started to come in, including one for £185,000. News got out about the rising prices of our chalet sale and we were shocked at what transpired.

A handful of people reacted aggressively and violently, demanding that we sell only to other Holtsfielders at no profit. We refused. Then a Holtsfield petition was organised asking us to keep the chalet sale-price down. Fair enough, we thought, and we made it clear that we were willing to listen and compromise. We assured people that we would not necessarily choose the highest bidder, but would try to find people who would fit into Holtsfield and sell at a price that would keep the chalet price below the market rates. But fears and rumours ran wild, and the situation degenerated into a barrage of intimidation by a small group of activists. We were verbally abused, threatened and confronted. There was talk of our chalet being burned down. Friends and acquaintances were contacted and 'warned off' buying the chalet. Strangers coming to visit us were stopped and asked about the nature of their business. Attempts were made to disrupt other projects that we were involved with. We asked the people concerned to stop; they made it clear that they would not.

Behind the scenes, other residents were disappointed at what was happening, and were working hard to restore reason. The situation was highly charged, the atmosphere was edgy and dangerous. Our children were being socially isolated, and the tension was affecting their well-being. We no longer felt comfortable in our own home, wondering what the next letter, phone call or visit would bring.

~

June 10th 2008, Holtsfield

"ENOUGH!" I shouted as I stood in the village green. We would not be bullied into a corner. I had been patient and tolerant and now I had had enough. I was raging! "BACK OFF!" I screamed. My head was hot with anger, my heart pounding in my ears.

~

We did what we could to arrest the situation. Gradually, over the following months, the wiser, quieter voices of reason held sway in the community and the situation began to calm.

It was a distressing experience for our family, and we were glad to leave. It seemed that for some of our neighbours it was a return to Holtsfield's troubled past, in which we had become the new enemy, and whilst it was only a few who held onto this notion, we were devastated by what had been manifested.

We endeavoured to understand how and why such a seemingly tranquil community had allowed such a vigilante campaign of intimidation to proceed in its name. I delved into the history of the place in an attempt to understand….

Holtsfield, along with several other local chalet communities on the Gower, was created in the 1930's as a self-build holiday park. At that time, Mrs Holt leased the plots annually to the chalet owners. The 30 wooden chalets were clustered around a small village green. The layout was simple and very effective in creating a strong sense of community. During the Second World War Holtsfield became a refuge for Swansea families when the city was heavily bombed. During the 50's most of the chalets had returned to holiday homes as the wartime occupants moved back to the city. During the 60's and 70's they became increasingly used as full-time houses, often by hippies. The occupants paid a peppercorn yearly ground rent and the chalets were bought and sold freely. By this time Mrs Holt has passed away and the ownership of the field had been put into a trust. In 1980 Mrs Holt's son, as acting solicitor for the trust, offered the land to the residents for sale. Then followed many years of fruitless negotiations. In 1989 Mr Holt gave up on the prospect of selling the field to its residents and sold it to his colleague Mr Jones who intended to develop the field and duly sent eviction notices to all the residents. Then ensued a long and protracted legal battle in which the residents united and fought to keep their homes. During this time of insecurity several people moved into the community to join the cause. In 1995 the High Court Sheriff, his men and a private security firm initiated a forceful eviction attempt. Having repossessed two chalets, the eviction was halted when trying to remove a family from a third chalet due to a turnout of approximately 200 people including the local vicar who had chained himself to the building in solidarity. Holtsfield residents marched to the House of Lords (250 miles) in March 1997 and in May that year the case was finally settled by a ruling from the House of Lords which granted secure tenancies to all the original residents who lived in Holtsfield prior to the purchase by Mr Jones. Those residents that had arrived and moved into Holtsfield after Mr Jones had bought the field did not win any legal right to continue living in their homes.

For the people of Holtsfield it had been a traumatic time that had ended in an uneasy truce. Neither they nor Mr Jones had won outright. The community had put their differences aside and united against a common threat. For many people the fight had simply been about stopping an unjust eviction attempt on their beloved homes. For some, however, there was an additional angle to the campaign, namely that Holtsfield was an exceptional place that had existed and should continue to exist outside of the capitalist housing market system. Whilst the community had come together to fight a common enemy, it had not been able to come together to reconcile its different perspectives, and redefine itself in common understanding.

For those residents who still harboured dreams of a cooperative Holtsfield, the sale of our chalet was another nail in the coffin of their ideal. For a few, our actions sparked a return to the old war, in which their homes were under threat. As experienced campaigners they were successful in raising a bandwagon. For the most part it seemed propelled by those residents who had joined Holtsfield in its darkest days, and whether this was because they still felt threatened in their own home security (being without legal rights) or whether they were motivated by what they saw as the common good, I do not know. When it became clear just how far they were prepared to go with their campaign, their bandwagon faltered and crashed.

We realised that our position was irreconcilable with some of the more radical perspectives being expressed at Holtsfield, and so we made peace with all those residents who were willing before leaving. In the end we sold to a local couple for £145,000.

I still think about the ethics of what took place. It was a time of great learning. I do have regrets, and believe we could have handled the situation better, and yet I acknowledge that as a family we were under great pressure. However in one thing I am very clear. It is far easier to begin afresh and create a structure for a new community, than it is to restructure an existing community. I have witnessed existing communities fail to restructure themselves time and again, even when faced with collapse. The same is true of physical structures. It is far easier to build an eco-house from scratch, than it is to make an old house eco.

Chapter 4
Lammas; The Conception

Natural energetic centres exist in our landscape. Each is unique and holds a particular resonance. The Tipi Valley area was regarded as a refuge for outlaws, long before the hippies ever arrived. The Clydach valley, where Brithdir Mawr was sited, has long been considered as a place of pioneers. It had previously been home to the self-sufficiency guru John Seymour, who inspired a generation of smallholders in the 1970's with his books. The Caswell Valley, where Holtsfield is situated, is a place of ancient resonance. These firmly rooted nodes of alternative culture are wellsprings of power. In turn they have generated and inspired new initiatives and ventures.

In the past I had discussed the prospect of a new ecovillage project with friends both at Tipi Valley and at Brithdir Mawr, wondering if there was a way in which the concept might be opened up to the mainstream and legitimately explored. For many years these ideas lay dormant. Then on August 1st 2005, whilst working as a circle-dance musician at Dance Camp Wales, a small group of us gathered around a fire to talk once again about the possibility of creating a new ecovillage. We talked long into the night and there was an edge of excitement and anticipation to that gathering which hinted at what was to come. It was there and then, under the summer stars, that the seed of Lammas was planted. Three of us in particular felt a new passion rise. Tone was inspired by news of an emerging new low-impact policy in Pembrokeshire. Larch, a lean young academic whom I knew from his visits to Brithdir Mawr, was keen to be an active part of a groundbreaking sustainability initiative, and in that moment I had found my path. A spark took hold that evening and blossomed into flame.

The project's name refers to that initial August 1st meeting. This date is the calendar equivalent of the Celtic harvest festival, Lughnasad or Lammas, which was an ancient celebration of the Sun God Lugh and the first grain harvest. *Lammas* translates literally from old-English as *first loaf.*

We formed a 'core group' to steer the project, making decisions by agreement. There were five of us to begin with and we made a good team. Chris, an information technology expert, created a website for us. Gordon, Larch's father in law, managed our membership. Tone, Larch and I provided the power, wisdom and drive.

And thus began my work. In the beginning the bulk of the work took place in the wee small hours of the night. It was a bit like sculpting a dream with energy, and then attempting to articulate the shape with words. I have heard it said that when one is in the flow of grace, then work is effortless. The work I poured into this project certainly flowed easily through me. I immediately took a driving position within the project, pushing the project forwards with unrelenting passion.

Having had to ask my teenage son, Jarvis, how to turn Hoppi's computer on, I decided it was time to become computer literate. I also bought a set of smart clothes and a briefcase. Ten days after that original meeting I had drafted the first edition of the Lammas ecovillage proposal. I quickly became aware, however, that I was going to need to make some changes in myself in order to communicate effectively.

One of my friends from Holtsfield, Helen Iles, was a documentary-maker working for the alternative film-production charity *Undercurrents.* She offered to make an internet mini-series about Lammas and the ecovillage movement with me. Thus I became a presenter of sorts. It was a role that did not come naturally to me. As a child I was always one of the kids at the back of the school play with one line to speak. I remember roles such as being a candle (hiding in a big cardboard tube) and a tree (hiding behind a cut-out tree). As a young adult I hated my picture being taken. Helen was very patient, teaching me how to be in front of a camera. I embraced the opportunity on the grounds that it would be a crucial tool for raising awareness of the project.

We defined our area of operation as West-Wales, and after approaching the various local planning authorities there it became very clear that our project was only going to work within one area – Pembrokeshire. The planners there were just finalising their County Development Plan and it included a new low-impact development policy. This seemed too good to be true. It was certainly an incredible opportunity. To understand where the policy came from and how ground-breaking it actually was I delved into planning history.

The foundation for the British planning system was cast in the trauma following the Second World War when the UK government created a framework to control urban sprawl and preserve the country's agricultural capability. The 1947 Town and Country Planning Act essentially divided towns, where people would henceforth live, from the countryside, which would be reserved solely for agriculture and forestry.

The following decades saw a revolution in farming practices which led to an increasingly mechanised farming industry and a decreasing rural population. In addition European directives encouraged farmers to focus on specified cash crops considered appropriate to their region. Forestry practices underwent similar transformation. These decades saw massive habitat and biodiversity loss.

In 1992 the UK Government signed up to the Agenda 21 action plan at the Rio Earth Summit, introducing the concept of 'sustainable development'. The scheme was designed to encourage joined-up thinking about the future direction of societies and economies, and in particular to focus on the conservation and preservation of environments and natural resources.

Meanwhile the concept of 'low-impact development' was launched by Simon Fairlie in 1996, when he wrote a book on the subject (Low Impact Development: Planning and People in a Sustainable Countryside). The idea was that there should be a provision for people to self-build environmentally benign homes in the open countryside in return for bringing about ecological improvements on the land and committing to sustainability.

The government's own commitment to Agenda 21 slowly filtered down to Pembrokeshire County Council.

At that time nobody really knew what ‘sustainable development’ meant. Pembrokeshire pursued its obligations by running two public meetings asking County residents what they wanted in terms of sustainability – one in the south of the County which passed uneventfully, and one in the north which was descended upon by activists lobbying for a ‘low-impact development’ policy. A follow-up meeting in Haverfordwest, organised by the Pembrokeshire Environmental Forum, and attended by Simon Fairlie, developed the concepts in more detail.

Several years later, to the surprise of many, a low-impact policy was floated and then subsequently adopted by County Councillors who did not appear to appreciate what it was that they were actually approving.

The forward planners within Pembrokeshire had taken Simon Fairlie’s work, along with two independent academic reports on the subject, and crafted a planning policy based on applicants demonstrating a positive environmental, economic and social contribution.

A unique combination of grassroots activists, enlightened politicians, and supportive academic research all being in the right place at the right time had led to an unprecedented planning breakthrough. Pembrokeshire’s low-impact policy was groundbreaking in its approach. The implications were enormous, effectively opening the door for a back-to-the-land movement.

The smallholding movement has, against all odds, never died in the UK. It is as if there is something in the concept of the rural idyll that holds a deep-seated appeal for people. Perhaps it resides in our genes; all our ancestors being well versed in the natural cycles and rhythms of life for countless generations. Many people continue to find living on the land hugely rewarding and nourishing. It was referred to as 'the good life' long before the 1970's television series came into being. Fortunately growing food, fuel and keeping livestock are relatively straight forward processes. Making money from the land is not so simple, requiring a very different approach. In fact it is very challenging to do this on a human scale, particularly in the context of a heavily subsidised agricultural sector. Herein lies the key to the success of low-impact development: its emphasis is on lifestyle, rather than income.

A conventional farmer will look at a field and assess the most suitable crop for that field and calculate the financial returns involved. A permaculture farmer will look at a field and assess what ecosystems would be best suited for that land, and would then work out what diversity of crops and thus what range of human needs might be best served with that land. The new policy was the first attempt by the planning system to embrace permaculture.

Pembrokeshire County Council subsequently launched a public consultation on 'Supplementary Planning Guidance' for their new policy. We jumped at the opportunity and played an active and successful role in shaping the policy guidance to create a workable structure for low-impact development.

I put away my woodworking tools and set aside my carpentry. The task in hand required different skills. I likened it to climbing a mountain. I put my head down, placing one foot in front of the other, focusing on the individual steps needed to make headway, rather than the scale of the challenge.

As time went on, the concepts behind our ecovillage project were developed in more detail and an unincorporated association was formed to take the project forward. Between us we had considerable experience of alternative communities, and we aspired to create a blueprint model that would bring together the best aspects of these, in a way that could be easily replicated if successful. The right people appeared at the right times and step by step the dream of Lammas was shaped. The project seemed to grow a life and a will of its own, manifesting the necessary stepping stones for progress to be made.

The initial concept drawing resembled a cartwheel in which 25 dwellings were clustered around a central village green and people's gardens and fields radiated outwards. The houses would be accessed by a circular track that would run behind the dwellings and would intersect the fields. Thus the village green would become the meeting point for all and would remain vehicle free. This model was based on the success of the layout at Holtsfield in generating a strong sense of community. We were aware that this conceptual layout would need to morph considerably when applied to a real landscape.

We spent a long time looking at examples of how much land people needed to support themselves and we estimated that each house would need to have between three and five acres in order to grow food and fuel, and to create a land-based livelihood to support themselves.

In exploring how many households we needed to create an optimum community population, we again looked at other working models for inspiration. We considered that eight dwellings was an absolute minimum in order to maintain an alternative culture. We noticed that a community can consist of up to (about) 25 dwellings, and when numbers increase above that level then notional sub-communities tended to form; Tipi Valley (with three distinct sub-communities), and Sandy Lane (with multiple clusters of chalets) provided good examples of this trend. We decided that ideally we wanted approximately twenty smallholdings to gain enough momentum and diversity to launch and maintain the project.

The settlement's legal structure was based upon the conventional village model, allowing people social freedom to participate in community if and when they chose. People would buy into the project and then could sell up if they wanted to leave. Households would thus be able to benefit from their investments in terms of land health, biodiversity, built structures and infrastructure. We were very clear that we did not want to create an intentional community in the traditional sense of the term. One of our guiding principles was that a family should be able to come and live at Lammas and never be under any obligation to attend a single community meeting, work-day or gathering. The framework would be as liberal as possible, provided that residents met the broad principles of low-impact development. This framework, laid out as a result of the planning process, would clearly define the legal requirements for both the residents and the organisation.

There were some elements that we considered best held in common: trackways, a village green, woodland, common grazing. In order to make provision for the care and maintenance of these in an equitable way Lammas would charge some kind of household rent that would cover such costs. It would then offer any employment firstly to residents, thus enabling people to make their contribution to the community in money or labour, depending on what work needed doing.

Our vision was that the land would undergo a transformation akin to that which Tipi Valley had previously gone through. Human-scale farming would shape the landscape, creating a diverse patchwork of forest-gardens, crops, orchards, and ponds with plenty of woodland for fuel, shelter and wildlife. The houses, barns and greenhouses, all self-built using natural building techniques, would merge into the landscape. We planned to create a network of permissive footpaths throughout the development to ensure the residents, along with local people and casual visitors, would be able to access the landscape and experience the benefits of this transformation first hand.

We had gathered hundreds of signatures from participants in Dance Camp Wales and the Unicorn

Camps in Dorset and used this to form a database of supporters and potential residents. Our newly created website enabled interested people to sign up and learn more about our progress.

We toured Pembrokeshire with a series of talks to launch the project. We were very conscious of our first obstacle: finding some land. Following our tour and the associated newspaper articles, we had a phone call from a lady, Su, who explained that two days ago she had offered up a prayer for people to come and work her land, and that she had the perfect site for us: 200 acres of south facing pasture in North Pembrokeshire, with a spring, woodland and a hydro turbine.

Tone and Jane visited the land and, whilst able to appreciate the potential, had strong reservations. On the one hand the land was south-facing, had all the elements for a hydro turbine system in place and a good area of woodland. On the other hand the land was relatively high and thus exposed to the weather, as well as being located in an area that had seen anti-hippie activity in the seventies.

I visited Pont-y-gafel farm and immediately knew that the land was right for us. I also had a lovely connection with Su.

Su, the daughter of a famous author, had moved to Pont-y-gafel farm 25 years ago with her husband and had set about farming Welsh Black cattle. After some years of hard work with little return, and following the trauma of the foot and mouth pandemic, they handed over the land management to a local sheep farmer and started a haulage business. Some years later they separated and Su was left with the farm, the children and a big mortgage. She was a visionary, and was unafraid to speak her mind. Her convictions were underpinned by a strong Christian faith, and she was clear that there had to be another way forward for the stewardship of God's Earth other than conventional farming practices, which seemed to neglect both the land's and animals' needs. Curiously the farm had a long history of having been radical and progressive in its attitude to land management, previously playing a key role in the cooperative movement. The lay of the land at Pont y Gafel suggested to me that it had previously been a hill fort. It felt like a natural energetic centre.

~

February 2006, our kitchen, 22 Holtsfield

I turned to Hoppi, enthused "It's as if the Universe wants this project to happen. We need people.....people come. We need land.....land comes. We need money.....money comes. We are being showered with miracles."
She turned and smiled "Yes honey, it's amazing. Stay grounded. Your turn to do the dishes."

~

For me the Lammas project was a largely intuitive affair that began in my belly, rose through my heart and was articulated through thought. The physical manifestation would simply be a consequence of the creative process. My core feeling was one of sincere gratitude for the opportunity to play a part in such a groundbreaking project.

~

March 2006, Bishopswood Nature Reserve, Caswell Bay, Gower

I was sitting at a favourite spot in the woods overlooking the sea;

"Dreamtime, dreamtime,
Wake up to your dreamtime,
With your feet on the Earth
And your head in the stars,
Dance your dream awake,
Dream your dance awake."

After some time singing, I listened to the sea and reflected on my situation. I felt driven by a purpose. Having returned to the fray of mainstream society, I was hoisting a flag, calling to all those who would listen, and then planned to carry this banner back to the hills. I was on a mission.

~

Lammas soon became 'Lammas Low-impact Living Initiatives Ltd', a 'Cooperative registered under the Industrial and Provident Society Act 1965 for the benefit of the Community'. When I first heard this term I was left with the impression of an archaic socialist institution. I soon came to realise that it was actually a very good legal structure that was part cooperative, part charity and part business. Membership to the Society was open to anybody who bought a share (£50). It was in fact the shareholders who owned, and thus provided, the foundation to the Lammas project.

Whereas previously the project had been managed by a self-elected core-group, with the change in legal status we moved to a larger decision making body and elected a committee of directors. Decisions were largely made by consensus, though we reserved the option to revert to a majority vote of directors on those occasions when we could not reach agreement.

Our intention was clear – we wanted to get prior planning permission for a model ecovillage development, setting a precedent which others could follow. We aimed to create a development that, whilst being rooted in the land, integrated itself with the wider community. Our reasoning was that the challenges currently facing human beings required all sectors of society to work together: individuals, families, communities, social organisations, businesses and governments.

The prospect of a new-build ecovillage had only been made possible in recent years due to society acknowledging natural limits to growth (such as peak oil and climate change) and embracing those principles which had for so long underpinned the alternative culture: principles such as sustainable development, living lightly on the Earth and natural building techniques. As a result of these leaps in awareness we were now in a position where both cultures, the alternative and the mainstream, had much of value to offer each other. To my mind Lammas was an attempt to fuse the two.

In choosing a site in North Pembrokeshire, we faced the added challenge of communicating with local communities whose first language was Welsh. Fortunately Larch had been learning Welsh for some years, and was passionate about its inclusion in the project. Welsh seemed more of a challenge for me. As a child I had spent school holidays with my cousins in the small village of Blaina, Gwent, roaming the hills eating blueberries. My relatives there were very dismissive about learning Welsh, calling it a 'dead language'. This, combined with the challenge of learning a language which was structurally very different from English, had so far dissuaded me from making the effort. I was beginning to reconsider.

I was also becoming increasingly aware of the huge challenge that would face the first wave of residents. Their success would be key, not only in bringing the project to fruition, but also in laying the path so that others might follow. They would need to build homes, barns, gardens, businesses from barren fields. They would need to do this whilst under scrutiny from planners, media and academia. It was going to be a Herculean task.

It was Hoppi's birthday when I took her to see the land for the first time. It was a beautiful spring day and the sun was bright. We walked across the land and it was a joy to see the blackthorn in blossom. I was a little saddened to find quite a few dead lambs' bodies being picked at by crows. It was not something that generally perturbed me, for in Tipi Valley the local farmers would often leave sheep carcasses to be picked apart by the foxes and birds. However the walk turned into something quite shocking as we found more and more dead lambs and ewes. In all there were over fifty corpses on the land that day, and many of them had clearly died in distress. This was not the introduction to the land that I had in mind for Hoppi's birthday. On returning to the farmhouse I enquired about this with Su, who told me that the tenant farmer did normally come around to load the bodies onto a trailer once a week, but he hadn't been lately. I was also told that he had recently been reported to the RSPCA, and that they had visited the farm and concluded that it was quite normal for there to be dead ewes and lambs at this time of year.

In April, Su, Larch and I invited all the Pont y Gafel neighbours to tea and cake at the farmhouse so that we could share our ideas for the project. About a dozen people came and there was a very mixed reaction to our plans. Whilst it was all very pleasant with lots of questions, in some people I could sense alarm rising beneath the surface. I did my best to share our vision with sincerity and yet I could sense sand slipping beneath my feet.

In the spirit of openness and fostering good neighbourly relations we followed this initial meeting with an open day at Pont-y-gafel farm, inviting all local people in the area to gather so that we might explain and discuss the project. Dr Jenny Pickerill from Leicester University, a supportive researcher, had been asked to facilitate the event, and we cleared out a large agricultural shed to host the gathering. As the crowds assembled it became apparent that many people felt very threatened by the idea of an ecovillage on their doorstep. A carefully planned program of working groups and feedback exercises was abandoned to the challenge of trying to calm an explosive situation. Gossip had led to wild rumour and wild rumour to a mob mentality. The loud antagonistic voices took centre stage. One Scandinavian lady became hysterical, claiming she could no longer sleep at night and accusing Lammas of raping her peace. It was difficult to reason with fear. We coped as best we could, though were left feeling shocked and disheartened. The open day had been an ambitious and perhaps foolhardy undertaking.

~

June 11th 2006, Pont y Gafel upper fields

I stood upon the pile of boulders and rocks and looked out across the land. It was early morning and the sun was beginning to rise. My heart was heavy with the weight of the project. My head was tired from the seemingly endless, thankless task. I let go of my thoughts and emotions, released them and was surprised by the wailing prayer that coursed through me. On and on it flowed. As I released I felt a heartbeat deep below me resounding through the land. A frequency lower than sound. As it rippled through the land it nourished my body. My prayer continued and the heartbeat quickened. A call and response between Earth and man. Some time later I walked away strong and focused with a clear resolve that I for one would carry on.

~

15th June 2006, Glandwr crossroads

Larch and I were sat in the car in awe at what we saw. The entire village was decked out in signs, posters and bed-sheets like some kind of mediterranean carnival. Except that this was no celebration of joy. The village, aware that we were having a gathering this weekend for potential residents, had plastered what seemed like every house in 'No Lammas' signs. We both felt very intimidated and drove through the village as quickly as we could.

~

It was around this time that the project came very close to folding. In fact, if it were not for a small delegation of local people making an impassioned plea for us to continue, we may well have done so. Spurred on by this pocket of local support, we committed to collating feedback from the consultations and seeing if we could change our proposals to accommodate local concerns.

Tone left at this point. He felt that his history as a planning maverick was jeopardising the project. This had certainly been raised as an issue by local people at our open day. In addition he felt a need to commit to finding resolution for his roundhouse planning saga, which was still ongoing. Whilst I understood his decision I was saddened at the loss for the project; his was a voice of deep wisdom in the team.

Thankfully Lammas held its course. This was as much due to a core group of committed, open-hearted visionaries, as to any ability on my part to hold the strings together.

Relations with local people in Glandwr continued to degenerate. I received a flurry of letters from villagers; mostly sincere pleas to be left alone. One of our local supporters phoned me with an account of a community meeting in Glandwr which, following a tally of supporters and objectors to the project, proceeded to exclude all supportive locals from the meeting so that they could work out a strategy to stop us. They formed a group and called themselves *Dim Lammas*, meaning 'No Lammas' in Welsh.

The local conservative MP, Stephen Crabb, publicly denounced the project. When we challenged him on this and suggested he might like to get his facts right before condemning us he took up our offer and, following a visit, issued a public apology.

Rumours reached us of a 'secret weapon' within *Dim Lammas*, someone 'on the inside' who would ensure we would never get planning permission. I dismissed such mumblings as nonsense.

~

July 3rd, Llandissilio post office

I popped into the post office on my way to a meeting at Pont y Gafel. Whilst in there a local farmer recognised me and, placing himself right in front of me, said "I don't mind you having rave parties; it's all the loose dogs I object to!" I explained that there was no intention to hold rave parties and none of us currently had any dogs. He left looking confused.

~

August 2006, Down to Earth project, Bishopston, Gower

The BBC reporter looked up from her camera, "And so Mr Wimbush, what did you do before Lammas?" This question caught me by surprise and before I had time to think about it I heard myself answer "I was preparing for Lammas." I was as surprised at my answer as she was, and yet it all made sense. The architecture training in Cardiff, the stamina required for tipi living, the farming skills from Brithdir Mawr, the surrender involved in family life; these had all been a preparation for this task.

~

Ultimately the adversity generated from local community relations led to a strengthening and a tightening of our plans. One of the biggest concerns of the local people was the scale of the project. In an attempt to hear and respond we split the development into two phases. We would apply for the first phase of nine households at this stage and would not develop plans for a second phase until the nine households had established themselves and satisfied the planners that they were providing positive environmental, social and economic benefit. We did what we could to address other local concerns, though to me the biggest objection seemed to be fear of change.

Having reached a point where our proposals were becoming sufficiently defined to give us confidence and clarity, we then began negotiations with Su over the future purchase of 76 acres of land. This in itself was a challenging task, in part because the tenant farmer was demanding a huge settlement payment to leave the land, and in part because of differences of opinion within Su's family. After many months of negotiations over issues such as road access, water rights and fair prices we did reach a place of agreement that, following Lammas getting planning permission, we would purchase the land at a set price. This was a significant step forwards for both the robustness of our planning application and also our own sense of security.

We erred on the side of caution when considering the size of the plots; allocating each plot approximately seven acres each. Thus, we reasoned, each plot would be viable in perpetuity even if occupied by a large family or if used for a spatially demanding enterprise such as grazing livestock.

We brought in a permaculture consultant, Looby Macnamara, to help us move from a place of spatial concepts to a well considered design for the site. She facilitated a series of design workshops in which we produced countless flow-charts and diagrams, considering the layout of the settlement from the many different perspectives: soil, weather, aspect, view, flow patterns for people, water flows, conservation, services, etc. This was my first direct experience of a permaculture design process and I was impressed by its comprehensive approach.

One of the aspects that we spent a long time looking at was our interface with the wider world. We were aiming to strike a careful balance between the privacy of residents and the needs of the visitors to explore and understand what the project was about. In looking at other models, an attractive precedent was provided by Holtsfield in which a village green, large picnic table, and notice board served as a community centre. The big benefit with this arrangement was that the ongoing inputs required were very minimal. On the other hand the hostel at Brithdir Mawr had provided a very user-friendly interface along with an income stream for the project. We knew that being the first ecovillage of its kind we would have lots of people wanting to visit. We reasoned that it would be best to make provision for these visitors and to create a mutually beneficial arrangement whereby we could generate some income, both for the residents and the organisation, in return for an educational and rewarding experience. We reckoned that a venue to accommodate this would become invaluable. We decided to run an architectural competition to design a 'community hub' and following this, allocated the contract to a Swansea based architect, Robin Campbell. Simon Dale, (a prospective ecovillage resident and emerging star in our team) and I worked over time with Robin to evolve and refine the design to meet our needs. The result was a turf-roofed, timber-framed, natural building which would be flexible enough to adapt to multiple uses.

We were then faced with the task of selecting residents. Up until this point we had simply gathered a lot of interested people and we needed to work out who would get to live where. This was important to establish because it was the individual plot management plans that would form the foundation for the planning application. Its strength and integrity rested upon the ability of the nine households to articulate their visions into a planning-friendly format. Given the amount of interest we had received from people wanting to live in the plots we were expecting a difficult task. We aimed to establish an allocation process that would engage people in such a way that if they did not get a plot, they would nonetheless be empowered by the process. No-one was automatically allocated a plot. Hoppi was very clear which plot she would like us to live on and we applied, along with others, with some anticipation.

What surprised us all was that events seemed to work out perfectly, in that we were able to allocate nine plots to committed and passionate people without turning anybody away. The process was designed so that by the point at which plots were allocated, everybody had made significant headway in developing their ideas and plans and presenting them as plot management plans. We had created a self-selecting process based entirely on the viability of plans and levels of commitment. This point is important to understand because it expresses the core distinction between intentional community and the traditional village model. At no point were value judgements made about people's personalities or lifestyle choices. As long as people were willing to work within the planning frameworks and were sufficiently committed to meet the paperwork requirements (which needed to stand up to significant scrutiny), they were welcome. The process of writing out the plot management plans had, in itself, sorted the sheep from the goats.

As a core group, we did not realise what we had taken on when we had begun the project. It proved to be nothing short of a bureaucratic mountain. At this time we were still based in Holtsfield and I was devoting about forty hours a week to Lammas. In the early days we had created a system whereby those people who worked on and coordinated the project would be rewarded with the option of buying a plot at a reduced price if or when we attained planning permission. As time progressed this proved to be an awkward point for some, particularly when many professionals and lay people alike were donating their time and skills freely to the project. Having invested the best part of two years work in Lammas, and having justified this to Hoppi with the assurance that we would be eligible for a reduced price plot, this was difficult for me to let go of. In the end the concept was abandoned for a system in which the project was powered as much as possible on a goodwill basis. This was a bitter pill to swallow. Fortunately Hoppi's own career, freelance training in emotional literacy, was thriving and she was able to financially hold our family. It was her support that enabled me to continue focusing on the project.

We continued to develop and articulate the vision, both through our website and by touring festivals with a display stand. We also held occasional gatherings which were an invaluable opportunity to communicate and get to know each other as a group. Whilst we did not have any clear expectations I think we were surprised at who the project attracted. People came from all over the UK, with an incredibly diverse set of backgrounds. Katy and Leander were living in a terraced house in Liverpool, with Leander working as a botanist for Manchester museum and Katy as a children's book illustrator. Ayres and Marianne were living in a first floor flat in Bath. Ayres, having previously been a US marine, now worked as a body therapist. Some people had bountiful experience of low-impact living. Many had none. People's reasons for joining the project were as diverse as their backgrounds. Some were motivated by the prospect of a better life for their children, others for the chance of an affordable natural home. One thing I learnt from this process was that you cannot pre-judge people, for they are often full of unexpected surprises.

The core group at that point started to fragment. There was a philosophical split occurring. Mark was a local authority solicitor who had joined our team for wholly altruistic reasons. He was a very intelligent man with a shock of white hair and dark glasses. He poured a huge amount of work into the project and played a really important role in defining a legal structure for us. He, along with others, did not want Lammas to assign plots at this stage, reasoning that the final allocation should only occur after planning permission. He recognised the need for plot management plans as part of the planning application, but felt that for Lammas to really work we needed to find the very best people from across the UK to occupy the project and to realise its potential. He felt that the best people could only be recruited in a post-planning situation. This approach was at odds with the way that I and others wanted to work. I felt that it was important to give those people willing to write plot management plans for the application our trust. I had faith in their ability to deliver. Both camps were acting with the project's best interests in mind. The meetings became tense and difficult. Things began to get heavy. In the end Mark left. This was a loss for the project.

Meanwhile we were tying down the way in which the finances would work in the project. This was challenging in that none of us had any experience of large-scale developments. Nonetheless, keen to install a comprehensive infrastructure network that would stand the test of time, we costed out the trackways, water and electricity networks as best we could. We anticipated being able to secure some funding for the community hub and hydro scheme and endeavoured to keep the plot prices as low as we could. We set the cost of a plot at £35,000. To put this into context there was a building plot for sale in the local village at the time; it was approximately one tenth of an acre and had outline planning permission. It was on the market for £130,000.

With the nine plots allocated, the hub design reaching completion, and the project's management approach laid out, we were ready to start talking with the planners.

At the pre-application meeting with Pembrokeshire County Council planning department we were told that our project would almost certainly be recommended for approval, and we were assured that if any challenges arose, then we would be contacted. We also managed to secure an agreement that our application would be assessed by people familiar with the concepts of low-impact development and permaculture, rather than conventional agricultural assessors.

After years of work we submitted our application to Pembrokeshire County Council on 1st June 2007. The planners had insisted on a printed application, with four copies of everything. It was housed in 16 box-files and delivered by wheelbarrow to illustrate the folly of such ridiculous quantities of administration. I enquired as to the progress of our case dozens of times over the following months and, on the rare occasion that I managed to speak with our case officer, was reassured that all was well. It was only on one of my routine enquiries five days before our planning application was due to be decided that I was given any indication of doubt. Three days before the planning meeting I received a copy of the agenda and was appalled at what I read.

~

October 9th 2007, Council Offices, County Hall, Haverfordwest

At the meeting the public seating area was full and the atmosphere was charged. A few of the prospective Lammas families had come to watch. I recognised some local people opposed to the project and we politely and somewhat awkwardly acknowledged each other. In front of us a huge rectangle of a desk was laid out and the planning committee lumbered into place. Largely composed of grey haired men in grey suits, they took their familiar positions with an air of authority. The Chairman called the meeting to order. The first item on the agenda was the Lammas ecovillage application. David Lawrence, Head of Planning, stood up and reeled off his lengthy speech of condemnation. It was carefully designed to undermine any support his audience may have had for the project. Wrong facts and figures added to the spin. Reluctantly he acknowledged our request to defer any decision, given that we had written objecting to what we saw as misrepresentation. He swiftly went on to emphasize that he would not make any recommendation on this, and that it should be a matter for the committee. The following speaker (our local councillor) in turn proposed that there be no deferment of the decision allowing us space to respond to the report, and that our application be refused immediately. The party to which he was aligned all fell into rank and in turn they dismissed the application as ridiculous. One lone voice spoke up for sustainability and vision. She happened to be one of the few women there. As she spoke, many other committee members scoffed at her in a shocking display of disrespect. The task in hand was resumed and the matter was dealt with quickly and forcefully. Eighteen votes to three. Our application refused. Two years of work discarded in ten minutes. We were not permitted to speak a single word at the meeting. My belly churned in disgust. We had been stitched up.

Chapter 5
Lammas; Barriers

10th October 2007, Preseli Hills, Pembrokeshire

The north-west wind, carrying a hint of the sea, leaned into my body. To the north I could see the small town of Newport with its long arc of sandy beach. To the south I could see the rolling foothills stretching into the distance with the blue-grey silhouette of Milford Haven marking the southern coast.
I had come to this place for some reflection. For me the Preseli hills were the closest thing to wilderness and yet they had, along with the entire landscape around me, been reduced to a degraded existence. Gone were the bears, the wolves, and the wild boar. Gone were the golden eagles, the beavers and the red deer. Gone were the forests, the flowers and the butterflies. In their place grazed a multitude of cloned sheep. I reflected upon a society that not only sterilised nature, suffocating it with a bland uniformity of industrialised production, but that also seemed completely unable to stand back and see the bigger picture.
I closed my eyes and opened my spirit to the landscape, refreshing myself with its ancient resonance. Feeling its history in my bones. Welcoming the wisdom of the ancestors.

~

On analysis, two main factors were cited as giving rise to the refusal of our application. Insufficient information about the project's traffic generation was the first. The second reason was doubt about the viability of the nine individual plot management plans, and in particular the business plans. We decided that the only way to move forwards was to use the obstacle as a springboard to better our plans.

So we upgraded our traffic management plans, and initiated a series of discussions and meetings with Pembrokeshire Highways department. We soon reached a point whereby we had their assurances that they were happy with our revised plans. This basically involved us placing a cap on the amount of traffic we would generate.

The second issue was more of a challenge for us. We had recruited people who were effectively pioneers. We had attracted practical visionaries with the power to turn fields into diverse smallholdings. None of us were naturally gifted at writing business plans and it was these that had come under the heaviest fire from the planners. To remedy this we were going to have to start thinking and communicating in terms of cropping areas, yields, investment costs and financial returns. Fortune smiled upon us once again and we were offered help by an agricultural business consultant. The key to negotiating the challenge lay in the form of an obscure farming publication called 'The Farm Management Pocketbook' by John Nix. For anyone interested in land productivity, this humble book will provide no end of statistical wonder, for example an acre of flax would yield an average of 266kg of linseed oil; a farmer can reasonably expect to spend four labour-hours per year per sheep to manage a flock; an ostrich skin is worth £40.

~

15th October 2007, 22 Holtsfield

Once again I sat in front of the familiar screen. Back to the drawing board, returning and renaming all those files that had been labelled 'final version'. One big sigh! "Is it all worth it?" I asked myself. I battled with the feeling of pointlessness and I felt tired with the struggle. I'd never wanted to work with computers and yet I was pouring the best part of my life into this virtual world. It left me feeling grey and depleted. Small solace lay in the hope that if we could get this project through the planning system then other people wouldn't need to reinvent the wheel, and could use our templates for future eco-smallholdings and ecovillages.

~

21st October 2007, Mumbles, Swansea

It was evening and dusk was falling. As I looked across Swansea Bay the wind carried a new undertone. The message was clear: 'The waiting is over. The time has come. Change is upon us'. "What more can I do?" I asked myself. I knew that we, along with our planet, were on the brink of environmental breakdown. The writing had long been on the wall. And I knew that the solutions were actually very simple. I felt frustrated at the seeming inability within our culture to address the situation. And once I had worked through my frustration, I was left with a simple choice – to accept and surrender or to challenge and struggle. I surrendered to the moment, letting the salty breeze push against my body.

~

Whilst the core group resolved to continue, the effect of the planning rebuttal on morale soon became clear. One by one, four families declared their intention to drop out of the project. To a degree the choices were influenced by individual changes in life circumstances, however the scale of the challenge and the prospect of another round of more paperwork and delays undoubtedly took its toll. Time and again we advertised for applicants through our networks. Then followed phone-calls, meetings, site visits, new business plans, allocation procedures and design processes. Three of the families had dropped out of the four-unit terrace which left us with a building largely designed by people who had left the project, and so we set about re-designing it from scratch.

The task of refining the application went on and on in ever decreasing circles. The individual plot plans went into even greater detail, the entire site being meticulously mapped out in response to the environmental challenges and opportunities that the land presented. Planting schemes were then translated into crop yield projections and integrated with the multiple business plans. Building plans were refined and infrastructure layouts reconsidered. The project sharpened its focus.

News reached us of another ecovillage project taking a different approach. Land Matters was a low-impact permaculture project of eight families in South Devon. Having begun in the summer of 2005, about the same time as us, they had chosen to simply move on to their land and fight a retrospective planning campaign. They had just won their appeal for temporary planning permission. Their strategy had paid off. “Will ours?” I asked myself. There were voices within Lammas that thought it was time to abandon the hope of attaining bureaucratic approval and simply move onto the site. Whilst I totally understood, I personally was convinced that we needed to stick to our original remit of getting planning permission before moving onto the land.

My initiation into the planning system had taught me that our application needed to be completely watertight. I resolved to go through all the paperwork with a fine tooth comb. Once again I put my carpentry on hold, and leaned heavily on Hoppi for financial support. It seemed to be the only way that we could ensure a tight planning application.

Occasionally I dared to look at what lay on the other side of planning and saw some fairly rough terrain. When we managed to get through planning we would need to buy the land and pay for the infrastructure. Then we would face new administrative challenges: funding applications, building regulations, annual monitoring reports. Then we would meet the physical task of building an ecovillage. The biggest task however went beyond these things, namely the challenge of not giving in to the voice of doubt and keeping the flame of hope alive. This was our greatest challenge and, if we got it right, it would be our greatest strength.

~

January 2008, the old monastery ruins, Bishopswood Nature Reserve, Gower

I was sat with my back to an old stone wall, facing the southern sunshine. I would come to this spot from time to time to contemplate. Nestled behind a bramble bush and enclosed with ivy it was a secret little place hidden from the myriad of footpaths that criss-crossed the valley.

Being at the forefront of the project, it was important to question my motivation. Why was I pouring so much into this? Was I trying to save the planet? I was aware that on a level of ultimate truth the planet did not need saving, the world was actually perfect right there and then. I questioned whether my motivation was in some ways self-centered; was I simply creating the culture and the landscape in which I wanted to live? I had spent most of my life getting very clear on where and how it was I wanted to live (as well as where and how I did not want to live). I wanted to live in a culture that honoured the Earth, and a landscape which honoured life and diversity. I wanted to live with abundance, beauty and music. I wanted to live here in the UK where I felt connected to my Celtic roots. And if that meant breaking the mould and creating a new model, so be it.

~

Whilst Su and her new husband Kevin were essentially supportive, there was mounting pressure from other members of her family to question the commitment to Lammas, particularly given our failure to attain planning permission. It seemed that once again the whole project lay in the balance. She had invited a panel of agony-aunt accountants from 'The Times' newspaper to help her sort out her financial situation. They couldn't figure it out; simply couldn't do it! For 18 months she had held true to her promise to us to hold the land ready for us. She had pinned huge hope on Lammas getting planning the first time round, and thus buying the land from her and going part way to solving her credit situation. Without a supportive landowner we were nowhere. In an attempt to tie down the situation and provide a lifeline for Su, Lammas offered to buy a legal 'option'. In effect this would be the formalisation of what had been verbally agreed; for a deposit, Su would guarantee to sell us the land at the agreed price. The project rested upon her faith.

We were aware that not only would we be breaking new ground in terms of planning, but that we would also need to create new legal mechanisms to reflect the structural arrangement that we were aiming to create. The plan was that Lammas would retain the freehold ownership of the land at Pont y Gafel. It would then issue 999 year agricultural leaseholds to the residents. This arrangement would enable the organisation to keep the project in line with low-impact principles, acting in effect as guardian. The residential leaseholds also better reflected the concept of land stewardship rather than land ownership. This seemed to us to be a much more enlightened perspective. We found a supportive solicitor who would help us draft the legal framework for us. Unfortunately she worked in Bristol which meant quite a bit of travelling for me. In the past when I have lived in towns and cities I have grown used to the urban landscape. However coming from a natural landscape the city appeared grey and dirty. I did not enjoy the trips to Bristol.

Sometimes I felt quite isolated in my role. Whilst there were lots of people working diligently away on the application, I took responsibility for holding all the strings together and at times that felt overwhelming. Each of the families had put together plot management plans. These documents included designs for the land and structures, business plans, prospective labour patterns, household-need assessments and more. In essence peoples dreams for a sustainable future. I knew that these needed to be completely robust and yet I felt a little uncomfortable sending people's work back with red crosses and scribbles all over it. It was clear to me that we needed to all be pulling in the same direction if we were to succeed.

~

8th February 2008, Bishopswood Primary School, Gower

At Jarro and Emba's primary school, a tipi had been put up as an outdoor classroom space. A beautifully painted lodge cover was pitched badly on a rather scruffy set of poles. The smoke-flap poles were missing and the lacing pins were an odd collection of twigs. Rubber matting had been laid as a floor. All in all it looked kind of sad. One day I took pity on it and, together with Hoppi, we offered to do some music workshops with the children in the tipi for a day. We borrowed smoke flap poles, brought in hay as a floor covering and mounds of sheepskins as seating. We created a fireplace with a circle of stones and an altar of crystals and flowers. We transformed it into a splendid scene. During the day we welcomed five classes of children in and we made ceremony and music with them. It was clearly a cultural awakening for many of them. The most interesting thing was the nature of the various sessions. The universe enters into a very direct dialogue with people when they are open to nature and more especially a ceremonial space. One of the classes had a fun, clear, light experience. For another the smoke from the fire was so thick that we had to abandon the singing. One of the groups was utterly spellbound and another was fascinated at the use of animal skins. They all loved the singing and music. For me it was a reminder me how far I had come from my past simple lifestyle in which I had a very direct relationship with the natural elements. I dreamt that night of starting a new life in a simple bow-topped wagon. A life of freedom on the open road. No planning, no paperwork, no stress. A simple life. What a temptation!

~

The resubmission date was pushed back bit by bit from November 2007 through to March 2008 as the workload grew. Coordinating the individual plot plans with each other and with the overall management documentation was a complex feat. It was important that the plans complimented each other and worked together. In some ways it was emulating the way in which Brithdir Mawr managed its land – encouraging a wide diversity of produce, though using individual enterprise as a motivator rather than the common-good.

Some plot aspects tended to be replicated, though reflected differing household needs – for example vegetable gardens and biomass-fuel areas. Some aspects were shared – for example, grazing, the woodland management, food processing facilities. The specialised areas tended to stem from the individual business plans – for example, honey, salads, mushrooms, pork or fish. There were a few areas in which residents duplicated enterprises and I encouraged them to coordinate their business plans and share distribution and marketing of their produce.

Other people stepped forwards to assist with different aspects of the application. Knowing that I was not working alone brought me a feeling of kinship. Kit, a prospective resident, dedicated himself to making a scale model of the entire project. As far as possible he used recycled materials. Whenever I visited him to discuss layout details, his overalls and hands were caked in a green and brown crust from layers of glue, paint and grit. Simon Dale was pulling together a whole range of threads from designing the temporary office and terrace to writing the woodland management plan and hydro-turbine reports. His skills had become invaluable to us.

We decided to submit the next application electronically and questioned whether to publish it online. This was a slightly high-risk strategy from the perspective of exposing ourselves to those people opposed to the project, but we were keen to make the planning decision process transparent. It's one thing to say "Trust us, it's a good application", and another to say "Please, see for yourself!"

I visited our local councillor to see if I could muster some support there. Whilst he could appreciate the value of smallholdings, having been raised in one, he simply could not understand how seven acre holdings could be financially viable when many seventy acre holdings were considered unviable even with substantial farm-subsidy payments.

The individual management plans finally reached a point at which I was happy with them. Su, after many months of negotiations, eventually signed the option agreement. We resubmitted our application electronically on March 11th 2008, with a copy placed on our website for the world to see.

My life returned to a more familiar rhythm. It was an enormous relief. I took on work as a carpenter. In the evenings I played music with Hoppi and at the weekends I took my children swimming. The Lammas workload dwindled to fielding enquiries from what seemed mostly to be media people or students. The application was with the planners. The letters of support were beginning to roll in. We were working with *Undercurrents* again to produce further episodes and these were becoming an internet hit. It seemed like we had a fair wind in our sails.

One of the things that inspired me to keep going was how the project had been such a team effort. Lammas benefited from a whole range of professional benefactors who gave freely of their time and skills. The residents themselves worked enormously hard, often contributing far more than just their individual plot plans. ‘Shareholders’ and ‘Friends’ of Lammas invested their money and trust in the project. When I stood back and considered it, Lammas had involved literally hundreds of people pulling together in one direction. I felt honoured to be a part of it.

It took Pembrokeshire County Council nearly three weeks to assign our application a case officer and number. Our previous case officer had since gone into retirement. Our new case officer, David Popplewell, was a younger man who seemed to be making good headway within the planning department. He gave me the impression that he was carrying a heavy burden on his shoulders. My initial communications with him were very disappointing. They seemed to revolve around him side-stepping and making empty assurances. The territory seemed depressingly familiar.

One of our supporters, Tom Wooley, advised us of a Welsh Assembly body called 'The Design Commission for Wales'. It was an organisation that provided a professional critique and assessed the calibre of new planning proposals. We submitted our application to them for review. They invited our David Popplewell along and after much pressure he reluctantly agreed to attend. We travelled to Cardiff with our new models. Following our presentation and some questions, the review panel expressed their sincere support for the project. In fact it was described by the lead panellist as "the most inspiring project I've ever come across in my time at the Design Commission." Their feedback would, in theory, be taken into consideration during the planning decision process. David Popplewell seemed very unimpressed.

Along with the resubmission, the anti-Lammas campaign in Glandwr sprung back to life. The group went from door to door across the local villages campaigning for letters of opposition. On a large blackboard outside one of the houses in Glandwr it was proclaimed that, following a local survey, 93% of the village was against us. The villagers hired a solicitor to lobby on their behalf.

It took thirteen weeks of lobbying before David Popplewell agreed to discuss our application. It was fairly pointless. He was not prepared to divulge any information other than that he wanted more time to consider things. I explained to him that we had been trying to open a dialogue with the planning department for eight months to no effect. He stated that "dialogue was not appropriate for planning applications."

~

July 2008, My Garden, 22 Holtsfield

I had been sat by the fire for many hours and all that remained was a bed of embers. The stars shone above me and a tawny owl called in the woodland around me. I felt lost and in limbo. I was ready to leave Holtsfield and yet there was nothing certain to go to. We had already spent three years on the project, of which eighteen months had been in a burdensome, bureaucratic planning process. I did not know how much longer this would take. If the planners turned us down and we went to appeal, a planning decision might take another twelve months. We might not win at appeal, in which case we would have to submit a new application. In my heart I knew that Lammas would happen; what I didn't know was when. I felt drained and demoralised. I was concerned at what effect these delays would have on the other prospective residents. The stress was beginning to get to me. The owl's melancholic call reflected my own despair.

~

One of the things I had learnt at University was that design was an evolutionary process that had a life of its own. As soon as you committed something to paper, it was history. The designs that we had submitted in March very quickly became outdated. Not only were we engaged in this disempowering process of seeking government approval, but the very game that we were being forced to engage with was by its nature too rigid to allow for any evolution. It had become clear that by conforming to the planning system we were compromising our ability to freely evolve. By fixing our designs at a point in time we were arresting our own evolution. I had begun to question how much we were able to affect change in the planning system and how much the planning system was going to impose change upon us.

We were first told that we would get a planning decision on June 10th. The planners pushed this date back to July 8th, then July 31st, then September 9th. David Popplewell, whilst easier to get hold of than our previous case officer, was very evasive, and seemed to change his approach to our application each time I spoke with him. Twenty letters of support from local people were 'lost', along with countless e-mails of support. It seemed that the planners were either incompetent or were bending their own rules.

As people and as an organisation we thought a lot about back-up plans and, time and again returned to a place where there was seemingly nothing else for us to do than to continue, come what may. The only way that we were going to be able to make a real difference to the ecovillage movement was to press on. This, along with the ongoing bureaucratic delays, led us to resolve to proceed to purchase the land from Su. That way if we got planning we would be able to begin development work quickly, and if we didn't get planning we could begin landscaping and tree planting whilst we went through appeal. This felt important from the perspective of keeping our sanity. It was challenging to invest so much energy into a future dream that may not come to pass, and the prospect of actually being able to do something physical toward realising this fantasy was important if we were going to have any hope of maintaining momentum.

As a family we decided to commit ourselves to the project, regardless of what the impending planning decision might be. Having begun the process of selling our chalet in Holtsfield we started to look for a house to rent in North Pembrokeshire. We both knew that it was time for us to move on, that somehow in order to really grow as people we needed to recreate our surroundings, to fashion a new environment in which to flourish. Nonetheless it was especially heart wrenching for Hoppi to walk away from our beautiful family home into the unknown, and difficult too for our children to leave their friends. In August we moved to a pretty cottage which overlooked a five-ways crossroads in the middle of rural Pembrokeshire. The cottage, named 'Eden', was situated on the crest of a rise and we were surrounded by fields and wooded valleys. We saw more cows passing our house than cars. It was a much needed contrast from Holtsfield which had begun to feel suffocating and claustrophobic. Our new neighbours were open and friendly.

~

26th August 2008, Eden, Llanycefn

I stood outside on the crossroads having just finished speaking with our case officer on the phone. I felt frustration beyond words. The urge to kick something very hard erupted within me. I eyed up my son's football which had, as ever, been left out on the road. It was two weeks to go until Pembrokeshire County Council's Planning Committee meeting. I had been informed that whilst the planners had already written their report, they would not give us any indication of their views at this point. If we wanted to view their report, we would have to wait and then arrange to personally view the files at the Council Offices 5 days before their planning committee meeting. I gave the ball an almighty wallop and sent it sailing high over the hedge into a field. I felt as if I were caught in some kind of bizarre game in which the planners, by virtue of knowing the rules of engagement, held every advantage.

~

4th September 2008, County Hall, Haverfordwest

We arrived with enthusiasm and anticipation. I was tired, having not slept the night before. We were ushered to a room with five large files of paperwork to look through. Simon and I hurried through the documents to find the all-important planners' report and agricultural assessment. We then flicked ahead to the conclusions. To our dismay the reports dismissed our project as unviable on agricultural grounds. We had met a bureaucratic brick wall through which we simply could not pass.

~

The committee experience was very much a rerun of what happened before, with an extra helping of anti-Lammas protestors with *'Dim Lammas'* placards filling the lobby. The dialogue between the councillors was even more scathing of the project, with our case officer being recommended for a 'bonus' for having to 'deal with' our application. Again, one councillor spoke up in favour of us and was openly ridiculed.

In protest we tied ourselves up in red tape outside Pembrokeshire County Councils buildings to illustrate and express our disappointment.

Whilst at the Council Offices I had been discreetly passed a note asking me to contact a certain planning committee member, and the next day I duly did so. The first thing he said to me was "You're new to this aren't you?" He went on to explain what really happens at the planning meetings. He described his position as sympathetic, though unable to lobby on our behalf because should he do so he would lose his long-earned respect, and thus power, within the committee. He described the planning decision process as entirely political and pre-determined. He explained that long before an application goes to committee the senior planning officers meet with key committee members to decide their response. The key committee members know that they have, through various political and social alliances, the backing of a large majority of the other members. To my disbelief he went on to explain that even if our case officer had recommended approval, even if we had somehow got a majority of councillors to vote for us, certain committee members would have had the authority to call for an additional 'full' committee meeting where it would definitely be opposed. He reckoned that we had absolutely zero chance of getting planning approval at a local level, having missed our opportunity to play the political game. I had always suspected that this was the case, but to hear it direct from the horse's mouth was an eye opener.

We decided to appeal to the Welsh Assembly. We had always been aware that this option would be available to us if we were refused planning at a local level, though we had hitherto been reluctant to embark on further bureaucratic procedures. We had reached a point where there was nowhere else left to go. The appeal process in itself seemed relatively straight forwards; more application forms, more supporting evidence and more delays. However, just as before, the planning refusal led to a morale problem. From the perspective of the Lammas residents, our lives were yet again in limbo. For some families it was becoming too much. For those who had already relocated themselves to North Pembrokeshire for the project, the situation was becoming intolerable.

Events then took a turn for the worse. Our request to appeal was turned down due to a technical omission on the part of the Pembrokeshire planners. Seven months earlier, when we had resubmitted our application, the planners, whose statutory duty it is to check that all applications are valid, omitted to require an 'access statement'. In fact they had specifically raised the issue at the time and stated that our application did not need an access statement, because it was a 'resubmission' rather than a 'new application'. Thus our resubmitted application had actually been invalid and technically we had nothing to appeal on. The only way forwards for us were to submit a new application and begin the whole process again.

Adding salt to the wound, the Head of Planning at the Council went on to issue press releases implying it was our fault.

~

21st October 2008, County Hall, Haverfordwest

I had been stood in reception for twenty minutes waiting for the meeting. David Popplewell had insisted we could only meet in the lobby. I could feel my frustration bubbling away inside me. How dare they treat us like this? People came and went through the air-sealed doors and the receptionist fielded her phonecalls. I summoned patience. I had tried to arrange to meet with the Head of Planning, though he refused even to talk with me about the situation. The large display boards in the lobby mocked me with their proclamations about the Council's support for sustainable lifestyles. A suited man walked in with sets of plans under his arm and approached reception. The discreet logo on his files led me to conclude he was a corporate developer. I wondered if he knew the nature of the system he was engaging with. He put his briefcase down and spoke to the receptionist. Moments later I was shocked to see the Head of Planning rush out to greet him and offer him a coffee whilst showing him to one of the conference rooms. He then scurried back through reception towards the canteen and caught sight of me. The look on his face was as if I had caught a boy stealing sweets – a mix of shock and cowering. Moments later he rushed back through reception with the man's coffee and avoided looking in my direction. Twenty minutes later our case officer met with me. We stood in reception whilst he explained that there was nothing he could do about the situation; we would have to submit a new planning application.

~

We were effectively ejected from the planning system. I felt defeated. A sense of hopelessness lingered in the back of my mind. I was not sure if I had it in me to begin the planning application process again. I was not sure if the group could withstand further set-backs.

Chapter 6
Lammas; Breaking Through

Life on the five-ways crossroads began to settle. The house, a picturesque traditional Welsh cottage with a lean-to kitchen extension on the back, had been built in the nineteenth century with thick stone walls set directly onto the bedrock. It had at one point in its history been a pub serving the Irish labourers as they built the local railway (now disused). It was a simple two-up two-down affair, facing directly onto the crossroads. The house itself was pleasant enough. The landlord had put in a considerable amount of work in renovating it, and it was fitted out with mod-cons. There was an oil-fired central heating system, a flushing toilet, a fridge freezer, an electric cooker and UPVC double glazing throughout. Its crowning feature, as far as we were concerned, was an open fireplace in the front room. The children were delighted at their new big bedrooms after the small rooms in our chalet at Holtsfield. They also really appreciated living next to a tarmac road, which gave them a place to cycle and play ball.

The disadvantages were that, like many old cottages, damp seeped up through the floor and down through the chimney breasts into the walls. This combined with the fact that there was no insulation at all in the building led to a chilly internal climate in winter, even when the central heating was working at full power.

It did not take us long to get to know the local people and this in turn gave insight into the nature of rural life in Pembrokeshire:
There was a local farming baron, Russel, who worked from dawn til dusk managing various patches of land in the area. He could be seen whizzing past the crossroads

up to a dozen times a day on various quad bikes, rusty tractors and old Landrovers with muddy sheep dogs running alongside to keep up. He owned a series of derelict farmsteads which were mostly used to shelter livestock. His trousers were held up with baler-twine and he had a jolly sing-song voice. He spent most evenings in the local pub.

There was the traditional Welsh farmer, John, who managed a small herd of dairy cattle on his family farm. He was saddened by the fact that his children were being forced to move away to the nearby towns leaving him without any help on the farm and was concerned about the long-term future of the holding.

There were the smallholders who tended to manage small flocks of sheep; some living in traditional farmsteads, others trying (with little or no success) to get planning permission to live on their land.

There were the middle-class retired English who seemed quite happy keeping themselves to themselves, thankyou very much.

There was a strong equestrian scene in the area, dominated mostly by women of upright posture, a firm manner and good strong hearts.

There were the woodland caravan dwellers – mostly people living discretely (and often honourably) on small parcels of land hiding from the planning system.

There was the local councillor. He was a retired farmer who, having already built a new house on the main road for one of his children, begrudged the fact that he couldn't figure a way to get planning permission for another of his children, therefore forcing them to move away.

And not forgetting the local gypsies who would cruise around at 5mph in a flatbed truck looking for anything made of metal that was not bolted down and guarded.

I used our move to a Welsh language area to propel me to begin learning Welsh in earnest. I practised with the locals at any opportunity. Nonetheless my attempts to put down roots in this place appeared to be constantly thwarted. I began to clear and tend the tangled garden, only to have it churned up by a big digger excavating the cottage's dysfunctional sceptic tank. I started to renovate a neighbouring derelict barn and had made the kids a play area just outside it, only to have Russel intersect the area with a new barbed wire fence and move two enormous bulls into the barn for the winter. It was as if I was somehow not being allowed to settle down there.

~

20th August 2008, Eden, Llanycefn

The rain pounded the cottage windows. The oil central heating was on full power more to keep the place dry than warm. I sat at the table waiting for the electric kettle to boil. Having recently returned from giving a talk in Cardiff, I wondered what the group of open-mouthed students thought about my hard-hitting talk. I had described how we were fast approaching an environmental tipping point beyond which there was no return. I had described how our ecovillage project was being held in limbo waiting for a decision from some 'authority' that would allow us to simply live lightly on

this Earth. I had tried to share a vision of hope. I doubted whether I had made any impact at all.
I watched as the cows lumbered past the window in their familiar routine. They made their way from their monoculture rye-grass field behind the cottage toward their milking parlour at John's farm down the road. Disproportionately huge udders swayed and dripped with milk.
"The show must go on" I said to myself, trying to muster some positivity. With a resigned reluctance I turned the computer on to begin work on the application again.

~

Attempts to dialogue with Pembrokeshire County Council were hopeless. We employed a solicitor and began to initiate High Court action seeking some kind of recognition of responsibility for the invalidation of our application. At the eleventh hour we received a formal apology from the Head of Planning and an assurance that our planning fee would be reimbursed.

On a personal level it was a very difficult time. Having just moved to Pembrokeshire in what was a high maintenance house, the pressure to generate some income mounted. We had optimistically thought we would only be in the cottage a few months while the planning permission came through. Hoppi and I quickly realised that we were going to need some kind of contingency plan.

After much contemplation I resolved that for my part I was willing to proceed with the planning process as far as possible. This view was not necessarily shared by all those involved in the project and discussions around this topic continued within Lammas, with some people suggesting a more radical approach. I personally was very reluctant to go down the direct-action route for a number of reasons. Firstly the whole raison d'etre of the project was to trailblaze a route through the planning system and to resort to direct action (and the inevitable retrospective planning appeals) would only be repeating ecovillage planning history. Secondly I reckoned that to move onto the land without planning would endanger the local support we had cultivated and would make future community relations incredibly difficult. I was also concerned that we would lose some of our residents in adopting this approach for, whilst some of us might be up for direct action, other residents had joined the project on the grounds that it had mainstream legitimacy.

At a push I reckoned we had approximately six months to get a planning result and if we were not able to show progress in that time-frame we would begin to lose people. It was incredibly difficult to maintain momentum within a project that's development had been effectively arrested.

So the challenge was to submit a new application to Pembrokeshire County Council very quickly that covered all the contentious grounds and then to try to appeal to the Welsh Assembly as soon as possible. The group rallied itself and set down to work. We put out a request for help which brought in a series of offers from a range of professionals and organisations. These were invaluable and we seized every opportunity to set about creating an overwhelming body of evidence that would dwarf the arguments that had been made against us. The planners' case, it seemed, rested on a conventional agricultural assessment of our application. From an agribusiness perspective our project was considered unviable. No surprise there! What most upset me was not the content of the agricultural assessment, but the way in which it had been commissioned and carried out. Way back at our pre-application meeting the planners had agreed that an agribusiness assessment would be inappropriate. They had gone on to assure us that any agricultural assessment would be undertaken by people trained in permaculture. The planners had then employed a totally conventional assessment from people who were not even familiar with the low-impact policy. Close scrutiny of the commissioned report revealed that the writers had not even visited the land. They had produced a desktop assessment of the project using the traditional 'agricultural test' reserved for applications for farm-labourer's cottages. We had to find a way of laying this argument to rest. We set about recruiting the best expertise available in the UK to evidence our case and then, in a lifeline of support for our family, we were offered some funding to pull the appeal paperwork together.

Two months later we submitted a new application. Now over 1500 pages and backed up with evidence from the most reputable agricultural/ permacultural research bodies in the UK. Within the application was a document called *The Process* that charted the complete run-around that we had been given by Pembrokeshire planners. It was a damning indictment of the planning system. This document, along with the rest of the application, was again made available online for public scrutiny.

~

October 2008, The Ford, Llanycefn

About a kilometre away from Eden the road dipped in the valley and crossed through the Cleddau river by means of an old ford. When I needed a break from the computer I would walk down and stand on the footbridge which ran alongside the road. I loved watching the river flow beneath me. Occasionally if the river was low and the light was right I would see brown trout floating in the water cruising for flies. I rarely saw any vehicles – the ford being too deep for cars. One evening a car did pull up and I met with the river ranger. He approached me suspiciously to check that I was not poaching salmon. I said I had never seen a salmon. I chatted with him a while. He explained that when he first came to Pembrokeshire twenty years ago the rivers, and in particular this river, were teeming with salmon. It was common back then to see up to forty fish in an hour. I asked him how many salmon there were now. He looked me in the eye and stated "In the last three years I've only seen one fish in this river."

~

Following the submission we initiated another push on community relations, trying to reason with local objectors and cultivate local support. For my part I visited the local town council meeting and tried to explain what it was we were trying to do. I spoke, albeit clumsily, in Welsh. Unfortunately there was still substantial local opposition to our project and it seemed to me that there was little we could do to allay this.

Meanwhile we were beginning to get savvy with the planners. Under the planning system, local authorities have a statutory duty to process planning applications within eight weeks. We were very clear with the planners – if they missed this deadline we would appeal directly to the Welsh Government without waiting for their decision. As this deadline approached, the planners requested a two-week time extension to process the application. 'Okay', we said, 'if you have all your reports completed, and you are prepared to meet with us, we might consider a limited time extension.' To our surprise they agreed. However the meeting was a false dawn and in it we were asked for an indefinite time extension whilst they sent off for more independent assessments and consultations.

The meeting did reveal the murky workings of local government. Politically the planners were under massive pressure from the Council leaders to block us as much as possible. However they knew we had both the moral and the policy grounds to justify our proposals. The planners were trying to be seen to be being constructively opposing the project and yet had little ground to work from. They were, after all, simply local government employees trying keep their heads down and do their jobs.

With no further delay we appealed to the Welsh Assembly Planning Inspectorate and the decision was taken out of the hands of local planners.

Meanwhile Lammas had raised over £200,000 in loans from potential residents and supporters in order to purchase the land. We had decided to move forwards come what may. We proceeded to buy the land and pay off the tenant farmer. We called the land 'Tir y Gafel', naming it after the river that runs alongside it. There was no turning back now. The act of liberating the land was a huge leap forwards for the project.

~

January 30th 2009, Pont y Gafel farm, Glandwr

The rain poured, gushing from the sky in torrential sheets. I watched as the tenant farmer, along with a dozen or so hired hands and helpers corralled horses into lorries. The sky was grey and the ground was brown with mud and water. Man, machine and beast alike slid around like novice skaters on an ice rink. The horses were wild and furious at their eviction and kicked at the lorry's sides. The farmers were rough, guarded and pissed off. The sheep had been exported the day before and today, being the day on which the deeds were to be transferred, it was the horses turn. I had come to witness the end of an era. The land had been managed by this tenant farmer for twenty-five years and during that period had been continuously grazed. One hundred and fifty ewes had steadily worked the topsoil into a compacted impermeable crust. A dozen or so wild horses had added to the abuse in recent years. No flowers grew on these fields. Sixty acres of degraded green desert supported little in the way of insect and bird life. The land had been stocked to capacity and had suffered as a result. As the last of the vehicles went to leave I went over to shake hands with the previous steward. We regarded each other coldly. Neither I nor the tenant farmer had much to say to each other. We were worlds apart. I walked the empty fields to check that all the stock had in fact departed and called our solicitor when I was content that the land had indeed been vacated.

~

A few days later whilst digging a trial hole on the land to explore the sub-soil strata I felt a sharp pain in my belly. Over the next days it grew and grew until I was having difficulty walking. I had developed two hernias which could no longer be ignored. The only solution was surgical repair. There was a six month waiting list at the local hospitals. I could not face the prospect of being bedridden for this amount of time – the implications on both family life and the Lammas project being unthinkable. I opted to travel to London and go private, where there would be no waiting period. The operation itself was relatively straight forwards and pain-free. After 48 hours the drugs wore off.

~

March 1st 2009, Eden, Llanycefn

It was a glorious morning with a blue sky and a warm southerly breeze. Leant against the door of the cottage I waved goodbye to Hoppi and the kids as they drove off. Jarro and Emba were dressed in traditional St David's day attire and were both looking forwards to a day of school festivities. After dropping them off, Hoppi was due to deliver some emotional literacy training in a primary school near Carmarthen. I hobbled back inside and gingerly climbed back into bed. From my semi-reclined position I took up the laptop by my side and began opening documents ready to work again on cross referencing supporting research documents for the application. After a few moments I had some kind of realisation that made me look at myself with some kind of fresh perspective. Here I was, propped up in bed in a damp gloomy room on a sunny day, my groin was black and purple with bruising and I was fixated on a computer screen, working on a project that many people considered to be pie in the sky, whilst my wife went out to work to pay the rent. I wondered if I was deluded. With some effort and considerable discomfort I struggled out of bed and, collecting a blanket on the way, slowly dragged myself into the garden where I lay down on the grass and rested. The presence of the ground beneath me reassured me that, whatever my mental and physical condition, I was indeed supported by the Earth.

~

March 15th 2009, Our plot, Tir y Gafel

Having grown frustrated with the limitations imposed by the recent repairs to my body I was determined to reach out and make some kind of mark on our plot. I wanted this first act to be one of thanks. It felt important to me acknowledge getting this far, even though we were still a long way from succeeding. With the help of our good Belgian friends Jan and Line,

Hoppi and I set out to collect and erect a standing stone in honour of the ancestors. Having previously been part of a team that erected a stone circle at Brithdir Mawr using stone-age tools I was very grateful for the tipping trailer that we recently bought from the gypsies. Using this in conjunction with winches and pulleys we were able to manoeuvre the stone into position with little physical effort. We dedicated the stone to the many generations that had come before us.

~

Now that the planning appeal had been registered we compiled and submitted our additional evidence and entered yet another round of public consultation. Once again we lobbied hard for letters of support, both locally and nationally. In due course we received a copy of the planners' statement of case. We had three weeks to respond.

Pembrokeshire planners were objecting to Lammas on three grounds. The first was that we had not provided sufficient information as to why we needed five years to establish ourselves. This was easily settled by referencing the endless sources of such information within the application itself.
The second argument was that we had not provided enough information regarding people's land-based activities to justify their functional roles. Again this was easily settled by pointing to the evidence, of which there was simply reams.
The third argument questioned the viability of the Lammas business plan, which had since been completely re-written.

The reasoning behind Pembrokeshire County Council's arguments was weak. I began to wonder if the planners had at last given up. The report went on to list sixteen proposed conditions. Aha, this was where the teeth were; the proposed conditions would tie up the project in so much bureaucracy that we would never get past the paperwork stage. The Council wanted us to ask for prior written consent to plant a primrose - literally. Under their proposed conditions we would have to provide eight sets of detailed evidence for their consideration and approval before construction works could commence.

And so once again, line by line, I reasoned and argued for viability, proposing what still amounted to a strict set of conditions, but one that would enable us to begin works without us having to wait for some new permissive process.

Along with the planners' reports came 91 letters of objection. I carefully read through every one. It was emotionally very upsetting. On the whole these were sincere letters from local people genuinely concerned for the future of their community. It took a lot of strength to work through and respond to the issues raised by these.

I was determined to make sure that every base was covered, and we offered the Council a legal agreement (referred to as a section 106) that would commit us to meeting our land productivity targets and not exceeding our traffic generation targets. If we failed in either of these regards we would be obliged to make a significant payment (fine) to the Council.

It was at this point that favourable news came our way. The Welsh Assembly Government had released a draft national low-impact planning policy. Being still open for consultation, in which we naturally participated, it did not carry much weight in terms of policy. Nonetheless it was a very welcome turn of events and a bold commitment on their part to support future low-impact developments. I dared to hope that after three years we might be on the home straight. We submitted our final arguments. The application itself was now epic beyond reason. It consisted of 51 reports and 27 appendices. In all it was 2,137 pages long.

A few days later I was once again floored with abdomen pain. At the time Hoppi was away training in Amsterdam and when it dawned on me something was seriously wrong, friends and neighbours came to the rescue. I was rushed into hospital, told by doctors that my appendix had burst, cut open, turned inside out, hosed down, re-stuffed and then sown back together again. I was in hospital for a week. It was awful. I could find no peace in the institutional atmosphere of the hospital and cried with relief when I was released. The stress of the whole planning battle was getting too much for me; my belly was beginning to look like a war-zone. And yet there was no turning back now – I had no choice but to see it through.

~

April 1st 2009, Eden, Llanycefn

I sat by the fire listening to the news on the radio. The political leaders from the twenty richest nations across the world met in London today. The world economy, dependent on ever increasing consumption of ever dwindling resources, had moved into recession. The meeting was surrounded by violent protests and one man, hemmed in by police barricades, died after being beaten by officers. World leaders assured us that they would pull out all the stops, giving it everything that they have; $1,100,000,000,000 to get the credit flowing again, to kick-start the world economy. And yet it seemed to me that they were clinging to an old-world perspective: financing mining, meat farming, deforestation, aviation, weaponry, car production, and banking. I could not help but see these events in the context of Lammas, where a small band of pioneers was being blocked by local government from creating a sustainable ecovillage. I sighed in sadness at the madness of it all.

~

The hearing date was set for 28th July and was to be held in the local town, Crymych. I was still in recovery from surgery as I prepared for the big day. It was the beginning of the summer and now that we owned the land many of the residents were feeling the urge to begin building work on their plots. Again there were voices within Lammas that were suggesting that we should simply all move on and begin building regardless of the planning system. We debated the many aspects of this in depth and resolved that we would allow families to move onto the land on August 1st. We would exercise our right to camp on the land for 28 days and we calculated that we should have a decision around the end of August. If we won planning we would then be in a position to stay living on the land and could begin building. If we did not win planning, then who knows – opinion was split.

The day before our hearing Hoppi whisked me out to town on the insistence that I needed to be wearing a suit the following day. That was the first (and last) suit I have ever bought. I recall seeing myself in the mirror and was surprised at how gaunt I looked following my illnesses. I had lost a lot of weight.

Theatr Gromlech, which doubled as the local secondary school hall, had been chosen as a venue. My belly churned with anticipation. This day was the culmination of four years work. As I waited in the hall for the proceedings to begin I was relieved to recognise a good number of friendly faces. I could also see a large grouping of local people opposed to the project sitting in a block on the left hand side. I was relieved to see that they had not brought banners and placards with them this time. The hall was packed to capacity (over 200 people) with some people standing in the aisles. At the front of the tiered rows the Inspector (Andy Poulter) took centre stage. David Popplewell meekly sat on the right representing Pembrokeshire County Council. On the left I sat with Simon Fairlie (author of 'Low-Impact Development'), Andy Goldring (Chief Executive of the Permaculture Association) and Rupert Hawley and John Gower (representing expertise in agricultural functional need).

The hearing began with procedural matters and quickly moved to the core issues. The Inspector took a professional and impartial stance as the debate raged. Some of the local people opposed to the project had prepared weighty evidence against us. It was like being on trial. Hour after hour of challenge and argument – verging on interrogation at times. The Inspector gave particular emphasis to the local opposition and seemed not to want to hear from our 'experts' at all. The local conservative MP, Stephen Crabb, sent a messenger who read out a statement objecting to our proposals. I had prepared carefully and I gave it my all. A few of the Lammas residents made impassioned contributions. By the end of the day I was exhausted and shaking with the tension, drained dry.

Two days later I had an email from a local lady who had been actively campaigning against us for years. She stated that whatever came of the planning appeal she wished us well.

~

Early August 2009, Eden, Llanycefn.

Sat around a crackling fire in our back garden with the summer stars shining down upon us;
"Wearing our long wing feathers as we fly,
Wearing our long wing feathers as we fly,
We circle around,
We circle around,
The boundaries of the Earth."

We sang to the Earth.

~

August 14th 2009, Our plot, Tir y Gafel

I was working on the leat above our plot again in an attempt to repair the drainage issues. The leat, a large water channel, was originally built to carry water from the stream to the millpond. It was approximately a kilometre long and was quite an engineering feat; carrying water along the contour of a steep wooded hillside. It had been lined with slate flagstones at one point in its history. Decades of neglect had taken their toll on the leat and it had become silted up and covered with an entanglement of brambles and young trees. A fox had at one point dug a hole through the bank and this now diverted the water onto our plot. I was clearing the silt out by hand when a bright blue butterfly came and landed on my hand. I slowly put my spade down and sat on the grass. We were there a long time before the butterfly took flight again. I gave thanks and in that moment I knew.

~

It was a sunny August morning at our cottage when the decision from the Planning Inspectorate arrived. The news that we had won planning permission came as a massive, massive relief. In the end it had all been worth it; the anguish, the despair, the long wait had all paid off. We had set a new planning precedent. My body slumped with exhaustion and my heart leapt with joy. Hoppi and I bundled the children into the jeep and hurried to the land to announce the news to those families who were camping there. It was euphoric. We could begin at last.

Epilogue

Following our planning permission being granted, the leader of Pembrokeshire County Council, John Davies, issued statements and interviews to the national media condemning the Planning Inspectorate's decision.

Along with many of the other Lammas families, we began working on our plot immediately – installing trackways, ditches and banks through the autumn and then planting trees through the winter. It wasn't until the following spring that I felt sufficiently recovered from the planning ordeal and the associated surgery to move onto the plot. We purchased and kitted out three small touring caravans as temporary accommodation for our family. Hoppi and I built our workshop, with welcome help from volunteers, throughout the summer of 2010 and moved in just before midwinter. It was intended to act as a temporary home whilst we constructed the rest of the smallholding, with our dwellinghouse designed to be the final piece in the plan.

In July 2010 the Welsh Government adopted the national low-impact planning policy. The policy, due to be in place until 2025, supports low-impact developments throughout Wales, whether they are single smallholdings or large ecovillage projects. It is called 'One-Planet Development'.

Throughout the summer Lammas sent invitations to local people offering free guided tours of the project. Feedback gathered from these tours suggested that the feeling of opposition from local people was being replaced by a passive support. Visitors liked what they saw.

For my part, following the initial infrastructure works I began the task of handing over Lammas' affairs to other people within the project. Having spearheaded the project for many years it was time for me to step back and for others to step forwards.

At the time of writing the Tir y Gafel ecovillage is still under construction. Barren fields are being transformed into abundant ecosystems. A human-scale infrastructure is being crafted from the landscape. It seems that the land is coming alive and that this in turn is feeding people in both a literal sense and an energetic level. The positive feedback loops are growing.

As is natural, further challenges and obstacles continue to arise in the project: infrastructure costs that far exceeding our estimations, a building regulations framework designed for conventional housing developments, the task of creating a fair and equitable framework for managing the ecovillage. In meeting the challenges that arise there are further tales of strength and wonder that are beyond the scope of this book: Simon Dale working every waking hour to coordinate a Community Hub build through the winter in order to meet a grant deadline, volunteers dedicating periods of their lives to shaping a new world that might inspire others, personal breakthroughs in pursuit of a lifelong dream. There will always be challenges, and these will always present opportunities. In my experience people are both resilient and capable beyond our perceived limitations.

This story is simply one thread in a majestic tapestry that continues to unfold with a grace beyond our comprehension.

~

An evening in spring 2012, fire circle, plot 6, Awel y nos, Tir y Gafel, Lammas ecovillage

We are sitting around the fire with a vast heavenly display of stars above us. Stretching away before us the form of our plot is etched into the landscape, with the trees around the millpond obscuring the lights from the other ecovillage plots. Drum, flute, guitar and voice weave a sensuous music into the night. Dreaming, creating, honouring and thanking all that has been, all that is and all that will be.

"Evening Breeze, spirit song,
Comes to me when the day is done
Mother Earth awakens me
With a heartbeat from the sea"

I sense the ancestors with us, silently communing with the music. In the valley to the west a dog fox barks.

Afterword

Our world is in the midst of radical change. We currently live in a society based on the ever-growing consumption of the Earth's finite resources. We have taken things too far and have caused irreversible environmental damage.

The challenges that we face as a global society are commonly accepted. Fossil fuels are running out. Precious metals are becoming scarce. Fish stocks are in crisis. Logging of primary forests continues apace. Soil health is in chronic decline. Freshwater is no longer widely available. We are in the midst of a biodiversity crash. The climate is changing. Sea levels will rise. Our societies will be turned upside down.

It is a time of reckoning. The truths behind our economic and governing systems are being exposed. Old wisdom is returning to the fore.

The Earth is a living being of immense beauty. The myriad of ecological webs which form part of her are complex and intelligent beyond our understanding. We have upset the delicate balance and have much work to do in recreating our society and redefining a wholesome relationship with the Earth on both a global and local scale.

Here in the UK we have inherited a landscape which has been fashioned by attitudes that emerged after the Second World War. With the best of intentions a planning framework which preserved our agricultural capability and contained urban sprawl was put in place. Our towns and our countryside were divided. Over the decades, economic forces have grown to create a landscape dominated by agribusiness and developers.

Yet the biggest obstacles provide the greatest potential for growth. In this reagard we are a most fortunate generation. We stand at a cusp; at the end of one era, and at the beginning of a new age.

Our greatest and most under-used asset is the land itself. I believe that eco-smallholdings have a key role to play in the way forward for our society, creating a more natural population density in which human beings live as a part of the landscape. It has long been an established fact that smallholdings are far more productive per acre than large farms. This is about more than just productivity though – that is old-world thinking. Smallholdings have the potential to create a healthy environmental balance for people, livestock and wildlife, reconnecting people with their landbase.

I see a future in which areas of our countryside move away from industrial agriculture to embrace an approach which is abundant and biodiverse: where natural homes blend into a landscape alive with the sound of children playing and birds singing; where a short walk in the country becomes an exploration of different habitats, crops and animals; where traditional crafts thrive alongside green technologies.

It is possible to live lightly upon this land. Development can be low-impact. Our structures can be beautiful. Farming can work alongside wildlife. Permaculture can feed us. There are alternatives. They are available now.

The first step is in daring to dream. The second is in trusting the vision. There is an abundance of support available if we ask; both seen and unseen. The world abounds in miracles. We are creative beyond imagination. The ability to remember the way home lives within us all.

Human beings are part of the Earth.

We belong to the Earth.

We belong to the Earth.

For more information:

Lammas/ Tir y Gafel: www.lammas.org.uk

Internet mini-series on low-impact development:
www.livinginthefuture.org

Tipi Valley: www.tipivalley.co.uk

Brithdir Mawr: www.brithdirmawr.co.uk

Tony Wrench's Roundhouse: www.thatroundhouse.info

To contact the author:

Please write to:

Paul Wimbush
Awel y nos,
Tir y Gafel,
Glandwr,
Whitland,
SA34 0YD

Lightning Source UK Ltd.
Milton Keynes UK
UKOW051420260612

195074UK00001B/40/P